Twelve by Twelve

Twelve by Twelve

The International Art Quilt Challenge

Deborah Boschert
Gerrie Congdon
Helen L. Conway
Kirsten Duncan
Terry Grant
Diane Perin Hock
Françoise Jamart
Kristin La Flamme
Karen Rips
Brenda Gael Smith
Terri Stegmiller
Nikki Wheeler

LARK CRAFTS

An Imprint of Sterling Publishing Co., Inc.
New York

www.larkcrafts.com

Editor:
Valerie Van Arsdale Shrader

Assistant Editor:
Thom O'Hearn

Art Director:
Megan Kirby

Art Assistant:
Meagan Shirlen

Production:
Kay Holmes Stafford

Cover Designer:
Chris Bryant

Prinicipal Photography:
Steve Mann

How-to Photography:
Deborah Boschert
Gerrie Congdon
Helen L. Conway
Kirsten Duncan
Terry Grant
Diane Perin Hock
Françoise Jamart
Kristin La Flamme
Karen Rips
Brenda Gael Smith
Terri Stegmiller
Nikki Wheeler

Library of Congress Cataloging-in-Publication Data

Twelve by twelve : the International Art Quilt Challenge / Deborah Boschert ... [et al.]. -- 1st ed.
    p. cm.
  Includes bibliographical references and index.
  ISBN 978-1-60059-666-7 (alk. paper)
  1. Art quilts--Catalogs. 2. Twelve by Twelve Collaborative Art Quilt Project--Catalogs. I. Boschert, Deborah.
  NK9105.T85 2011
  746.46092'2--dc22

                            2010030796

10 9 8 7 6 5 4 3 2 1

First Edition

Published by Lark Crafts
An Imprint of Sterling Publishing Co., Inc.
387 Park Avenue South, New York, NY 10016

Text © 2011, Deborah Boschert, Gerrie Congdon, Helen L. Conway, Kirsten Duncan, Terry Grant, Diane Perin Hock, Françoise Jamart, Kristin La Flamme, Karen Rips, Brenda Gael Smith, Terri Stegmiller, Nikki Wheeler
Photography © 2011, Lark Crafts, an Imprint of Sterling Publishing Co., Inc., unless otherwise specified
Illustrations © 2011, Lark Crafts, an Imprint of Sterling Publishing Co., Inc., unless otherwise specified

Distributed in Canada by Sterling Publishing,
c/o Canadian Manda Group, 165 Dufferin Street
Toronto, Ontario, Canada M6K 3H6

Distributed in the United Kingdom by GMC Distribution Services,
Castle Place, 166 High Street, Lewes, East Sussex, England BN7 1XU

Distributed in Australia by Capricorn Link (Australia) Pty Ltd.,
P.O. Box 704, Windsor, NSW 2756 Australia

If you have questions or comments about this book, please contact:
Lark Crafts
67 Broadway
Asheville, NC 28801
828-253-0467

Manufactured in China

ISBN 13: 978-1-60059-666-7

For information about custom editions, special sales, premium and corporate purchases, please contact Sterling Special Sales Department at 800-805-5489 or specialsales@sterlingpub.com.

For information about desk and examination copies available to college and university professors, requests must be submitted to academic@larkbooks.com. Our complete policy can be found at www.larkcrafts.com.

Contents

How Twelve by Twelve Came to Be

For many of us, it is difficult to think about quilting without conjuring up a mental image that involves a group of people. Those who aren't actively involved in quilting tend to imagine a group of white-haired ladies seated around a hand-quilting frame. But those of us who define ourselves as quilters and artists probably have a broader assortment of images in mind. We might picture our quilt guilds or mini-groups, the people we've met in workshops, the friends who accompany us on our fabric buying sprees, or the artists

Blowin' in the Wind
Diane Perin Hock

who share their work in our critique groups. Many quilters I know imagine their grandmothers and aunts and mothers, knowing that they are continuing along a thread-strewn family path. Even quilters who don't have others around them know that they belong to a long and wonderful

tradition of women creating something new and beautiful from scraps of fabric. While we work alone in our studios, we know we are part of a bigger community.

I didn't realize it at the time, but in retrospect I think I was spurred to start our group (technically called the Twelve by Twelve Collaborative Art Quilt Project) by a search for my own art quilting community. Over Labor Day weekend in 2007, I attended a quilt show in my area and was entranced by a set of quilts that was exhibited there. A mini-group of six members based in Marin County, California, had challenged each other to make small quilts on a monthly basis, following a theme each member selected in turn. I enjoyed looking at each piece on its own merits, but what really fascinated me was how each artist had interpreted the same theme in her own way. The collection of quilts sparked my

Chocolate Desire
Nikki Wheeler

imagination and immediately made me wish I had a group of fellow artists with whom to share such a fun exploration.

Brunswick Street
Kirsten Duncan

Nowadays, the concept of "journal quilts" is widely known—many quilt artists have challenged themselves to make weekly or monthly small quilts on selected topics, sharing them via mini-groups, magazines, and blogs. At the time, however, the idea was not a widespread one. I loved the notion, but I knew myself well enough to know that I wouldn't follow through with monthly quilt-making without some external motivation. As a friend reminded me recently, a deadline is just an opportunity to finish something! I realized that if I pulled together a group of fiber artists to participate with me and produce work on set deadlines, I'd be much more inclined to keep with it.

I'd begun blogging in 2004—yet another vehicle for finding and participating in a community of quilters. While I found lots of knitters and general crafters writing blogs then, I was not able to find many blogs by art quilters. That gap led me to organize the Artful Quilters Blog Ring as a way to link art quilters who wrote about their fiber art online. Through the ring, I became acquainted with art quilters all over the world, and it was part of my daily routine to check in to various blogs to see what my favorite artists were doing. Inspiration struck when it occurred to me that I could invite some of my favorite blogging art quilters to join me in an ongoing challenge. With the Internet as our forum, we could be anywhere in the world and still share our work and our ideas.

Droplets
Françoise Jamart

Radiance
Brenda Gael Smith

So that's what I did. I made up a list of the artists whose work inspired me and blogs entertained me, and I sent them invitations via e-mail. I proposed the general idea of an ongoing small-quilt challenge group, with the details to be worked out later. I'd only met two of the women in person previously; the others were artists I'd never seen face to face, but felt I'd come to know through work I loved and blog writing that was charmingly personal. I was delighted when these 11 women signed on.

So there we were: Brenda Gael Smith in Copacabana, Australia; Deborah Boschert in Lewisville, Texas; Kristin LaFlamme in Waipahu, Hawaii (though in Germany at the time); Gerrie Congdon and Terry Grant in Portland, Oregon; Kirsten Duncan in Townsville, Australia; Françoise Jamart in Louvain-la-Neuve, Belgium; Nikki Wheeler in Poulsbo, Washington; Helen L. Conway in St. Helens, United Kingdom; Terri Stegmiller in

Mandan, North Dakota; Karen Rips in Thousand Oaks, California; and me, Diane Perin Hock, in Healdsburg, California. We were scattered around the globe, but all eager to try a collaborative art quilting challenge.

Via e-mail, we agreed on a schedule and a loose set of guidelines. We decided that each piece would be 12 by 12 inches (30.5 x 30.5 cm) in size, and that we'd give ourselves 60 days

Lost City
Karen Rips

to work on each piece. We agreed that we'd have a challenge theme, which each artist could interpret any way she chose as long as she could articulate how the word or concept provided the springboard to her creation. We set no limits on techniques and materials, although we agreed to the concept of "quilt" as including three layers. We set up a blog to discuss our challenges, and away we went.

THE TWELVE THEMES

To start things off, I named Dandelion as our first theme. E-mails and blog entries flew back and forth as we pondered the imagery that word evoked, and suddenly we noticed dandelions everywhere we went. Our first deadline fell on November 1, which we eventually revised to encompass the range of dates between October 30 and November 2 to accommodate our different time zones. The suspense was tangible as the deadline approached, and we were all so eager that we ended up revealing our quilts on October 30.

Change
Helen L. Conway

When I logged onto my computer that morning, several of the quilts had already been posted and I was beside myself with excitement. I gasped with delight as I saw the different approaches each of us had taken to the same theme. Each time I refreshed my computer screen, another entry appeared on the blog. All of that day and the next, I returned to the blog to admire the pieces and read everyone's entries and comments. I just couldn't stop grinning over how wonderful it was to connect with these artists and see how beautiful the work was.

Salvaged Chairs
Gerrie Congdon

Our challenges proceeded with new themes and entries every other month. We've come to know each other much better, and have developed true friendships from our distant locations. Some of us have

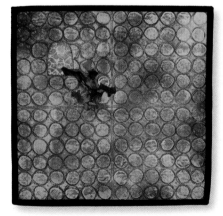

Defenestration
Kristin La Flamme

been lucky enough to meet up with other Twelves on our travels, and we fantasize about a Twelve by Twelve retreat together. (Now that Kristin

Identity X9
Terri Stegmiller

lives in Hawaii, her home is a popular choice!) Our day-to-day lives are quite different—we have different careers and family obligations; we may be caretakers to children and parents and spouses; we are active in our communities and quilt guilds and art groups. But we share a love of color and design, and we all relished the prospect of taking on each new challenge topic and interpreting it with fabric and thread. I think we all enjoyed trying to guess what each of us would do as every new challenge was revealed. We recognize each other's styles now, but I suspect that we rarely failed to surprise and delight one another. From comments on the blog, we also learned that other fiber artists started their own groups or played along with us on our posted challenge themes.

We are delighted to present our challenge project in book form. Each of our challenge themes is explored in depth with a focus on one work from each challenge, written by the artist who made the feature quilt. We also share images of all of the quilts that were created for that theme with brief comments by the artists who made them. (We give a nod to the Twelve who chose the theme, too. On a couple of occasions, the artist who chose the theme is the same Twelve who wrote the text.) Each chapter reflects the personality of the quilt artist who wrote it, and none discuss exactly the same things. But we hope this approach shows how each of us as individuals addressed the challenges, as well as how we as a group explored a common theme.

Passion & Pain
Terry Grant

I anticipated that the Twelve by Twelve challenges would be a lot of fun. But I did not anticipate the depth of inspiration and friendship I

Seven Houses Five Trees
Deborah Boschert

would find through this process. As we've gathered together—in a virtual way—to share our passion for art quilting, we've formed bonds that encompass more than just the artwork we create. Like those ladies at the quilting frame years ago, we're using the technology at hand to create a quilting community for our own time. The success of our group highlights the fact that now, more than ever, any quilter who wants to can find or create a community of like-minded people. Whether we know each other or not, whether we're neighborhood friends or we've never seen each other, we continue to delight each other through the work we do. Just as our project was inspired by another group of artists and as we know that we inspire each other, we hope that we can in turn inspire others with the results of our collaboration.

—Diane Perin Hock

Visit the Twelve by Twelve website and blog: www.Twelveby12.org

As I thought of ideas for the first Twelve by Twelve challenge, my objective was to select a theme that was sufficiently specific so our pieces would be immediately cohesive, but that was also broad enough to encompass a variety of images.

Dandelion Construction

Ubiquitous

Where Does All The Yellow Go?

There Wasn't Even Time to Say Goodbye

Weeds Are Flowers Too

Blowin' in the Wind

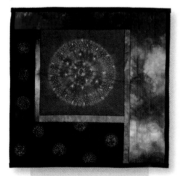

Dandelions

Löwenzahn und Pusteblume

Summer Scourge

Pièce de Résistance

Ferocious Dan

Dandelion Wine

Blowin' in the Wind

Diane Perin Hock

I recalled a workshop I'd taken with the master of abstracting natural flora, Jane Sassaman. "What do you want to say about that flower?" she'd asked me, as I struggled to design a quilt around a fuchsia blossom. She had reminded me that I had choices to make about what aspects of the flower I portrayed and how I portrayed it, and it was up to me to emphasize the parts I wanted to feature.

Diane Perin Hock

My Quilting Life

When I think back, my earliest memories are of fabric...the floral upholstery on my grandmother's couch, a particular gray-and-yellow plaid wool skirt I wore as a toddler. When my grandmother showed me how to use her treadle sewing machine, I was in heaven. The box of fabric scraps given to my sister and me by a friend of my non-sewing mother was like treasure, and we endlessly entertained ourselves with it. So I guess it's fair to say that it was the love of fabric that brought me to quilting. There's something about combining patterns and colors that I find fascinating, fun, and always satisfying.

I first learned to quilt in what I call the "PRC" era, that is, "pre-rotary cutting." Yes, I cut squares out of cardboard and marked every single piece to cut them out individually with scissors—without a great deal of precision, I'm afraid. I wasn't daunted, though, and made several quilts for friends and family members. Working in a fabric store during my college years taught me a lot about how to look at fabric and envision a final product, and how to assemble a successful assortment of fabrics. My favorite job in the store was helping customers select the fabrics for their quilts. I couldn't believe I got paid to have that much fun.

For a time, I let Real Life intervene in all that fabric fun, however. Law school, legal practice, marriage, and a child consumed my time and energy. It wasn't until my daughter entered pre-school and the staff asked for volunteers to

Dandelion Construction

A couple of years ago, I had a lovely conversation with a woman who took pictures of dandelions on her travels all around the world. She said they are everywhere. I thought of that as I created this quilt. A little shrine composition seems appropriate to raise the stature of the lowly weed. At the beginning of our Twelve by Twelve journey, I incorporated some of my favorite elements: handwriting, paint, hand embroidery, and a bit of embellishment.

Deborah Boschert

make an auction quilt that I returned to quilting. What a surprise that was! Rotary cutters and mats had hit the market, and the fabric choices simply delighted me. I'll never forget picking up Freddy Moran's book, *Freddy's House*. The use of vivid colors and wild patterns to create contemporary quilts out of traditional quilt patterns just thrilled me. I swear, Freddy Moran's book changed my life. The scraps from that auction quilt formed the start of a stash that now overflows my closet, and I've been immersed in quilting ever since.

I make both art quilts and bed quilts, and usually have an assortment of projects going simultaneously. I like to have something that suits my mood at any given time, so that I have projects available depending on how mindlessly (or mindfully) I

want to work. I have projects sitting in my closet because I'm mulling over where to go next on them; I'll get to them eventually, I know. Right now I'm working on a piece I started three years ago, and only recently did I decide on the right technique for finishing it. For me, making a quilt is more about the process than it is about having the completed project.

The Twelve by Twelve project has been a great push for me, as I suspected it would. Having a deadline every other month has pushed me to create, even at times when other aspects of life are demanding and I might not otherwise let myself play with fabric. I'm always glad that I took the time to do it, and I'm reminded over and over that the time I spend working on fiber art refreshes and refuels me in other aspects of

my life. It has been especially helpful to have to work in a small format, which is not something I generally do. Whenever I've started a piece with the idea to work small, it has immediately grown larger, as if the size takes on a life of its own. The 12 x 12-inch (30.5 x 30.5-cm) format of these challenges has forced me to think and work in a very different, and more disciplined, way.

My quilting space is a small bedroom in our home that doubles as a studio and an office for the legal work I do from home. One side of the room contains my desk, computer, and files, and the other holds my sewing table and machine. The closet is stuffed to the gills with fabric, paints, and other supplies, and my shelves are full of quilting books that I return to frequently for

Ubiquitous

I enjoyed making this piece about the maligned dandelion. I took a close-up photo of a dandelion that had gone to seed. Using photo-imaging software, I created a black-and-white image in three different sizes, from which I created Thermofax screens. Using a chlorine-based cleanser, I discharged the images on a base of overdyed cotton. I hand-stitched the dandelions with variegated hand-dyed perle cotton.

inspiration. While I am envious of the large studios I know some of the other Twelves have (with dedicated wet and dry spaces, even! Oh, the luxury!), I feel lucky to have a room where I can keep my sewing machine out all of the time and just close my door on the mess when I'm not working. I take over the kitchen table for projects that require a large surface, and I dye fabric out on our backyard patio with our black Lab, Gemma, underfoot. Some day, I'll have a larger space, but for now my studio/office works for me.

Where Does All The Yellow Go?

All my fellow Twelves were blogging pretty photos of dandelions in fields and I was stuck in an inner-city area of London, working. There were no dandelions! Or flowers of any kind. In fact, there wasn't even anything obviously dandelion colored. Where did all the yellow go? I realized that in cities, yellow is limited to warnings of danger. The photos of street furniture in this quilt were taken in Leeds on my next trip. I found perfect petal-shaped buttons at a quilt show in Harrogate. This is truly a cosmopolitan quilt. The title question also applies to the flower as it changes from petal to "puffball," and I quilted dandelion shapes in monofilament to represent this transformation. Even in the city, beauty can be found.

Helen L Conway

Choosing the Theme

Admittedly, it can be a bit daunting to choose a theme when you know that other artists are going to invest time and energy working on it. I hadn't yet discovered how imaginative and clever the Twelves are regardless of the topic in front of them, or how readily they find interpretations that would never occur to me.

One of the goals in my own artwork is to portray humble and ordinary things in an extraordinary and artful way. That concept was my starting point in thinking about a challenge topic, and as I thought about the ordinary things that each of us would encounter despite our

There Wasn't Even Time to Say Goodbye

At first I wanted to capture the point in a dandelion's development when the seeds are just hanging on, almost ready to fly but not quite. As I daydreamed and thought, R.E.M.'s song "Wendell Gee" was in high rotation on my playlist and suddenly the seeds took flight. There was the moment I needed to record—seeds scattering, drifting wherever the wind blew, an image of abandon, release, and freedom.

Kirsten Duncan

Exploring the Theme

different settings, somewhere along the way I started thinking about leaves. That thought led naturally to dandelions, which I've always loved for their vibrant yellow blooms, their fairy-wish puffs, their spiky green leaves, and their relentless persistence despite all efforts to eradicate them. As soon as I thought "dandelion," I knew I'd found my topic.

Even though I was the one to choose the theme, I didn't have a specific idea in mind and I didn't get to work right away. My first step was to look for pictures of dandelions in various forms. As luck would have it, our lawn had just been mowed and there were no dandelions in sight in the yard. I turned, as I often do, to Google Images and Flickr, both excellent resources for sparking ideas and inspiration. (Because of copyright laws, I do not use images I find there as a direct source for my artwork unless I receive express permission from the image's creator.) Inspired by the huge variety of dandelion images, I pulled out my sketchbook and started drawing. The squarish ends of the dandelion

petals caught my attention, as did the dramatic spears of foliage. I drew abstract dandelion puffs, mere lines and circles, to see where those led me.

I brainstormed word associations with "dandelion." I jotted "yellow," "jaunty," "weed," "cheery," "transformation," "float," "wind," "cloud," and other ideas that came to mind.

I recalled a workshop I'd taken with the master of abstracting natural flora, Jane Sassaman. "What do you want to say about that flower?" she'd asked me as I struggled to design a quilt around a fuchsia blossom. She had reminded me that I had choices to make about what aspects of the flower I portrayed and how I portrayed it, and it was

Weeds Are Flowers Too

Once I discarded a much-too-complicated dandelion design, I knew that I wanted to focus in very closely on just one blossom. Partway into the construction it occurred to me to add the bee, which became my favorite part of the piece. I used commercial prints, which I painted to achieve a dimensional look. The design is fused and machine quilted.

Terry Grant

up to me to emphasize the parts I wanted to feature. So, I asked myself that question: What did I want to say about dandelions? The more I thought about dandelions, the more I realized that my favorite aspect of them is their delicate white puffs, and I decided that I wanted my piece to feature them. I made rough (very rough!) thumbnail sketches of different layouts until I settled on a layout that I wanted to use.

I thought about how dandelions in puff form create polka dots of white on a green field of grass, and I experimented a bit using bleach to discharge circles of white from green hand-dyed fabric. In my imagination, the effect was ethereal and spectacular. In reality, I got heavy-looking off-white blobs that disappointed me. I set that aside and moved on. I tried thread-painting, scribbling lines of white thread on green fabric. Again, the result was disappointing, and I tossed those pieces into the trash.

Still experimenting, I hooked up the needle-felting attachment I'd recently bought for my sewing machine. A needle felting machine or attachment does not use thread in the top or bobbin of the machine. Instead of a typical sewing machine needle, it has several finely barbed needles that punch through and slightly shred the edges of whatever fibers you expose to the needles. When you layer one fabric on top of another, the repeated action of the

Dandelions

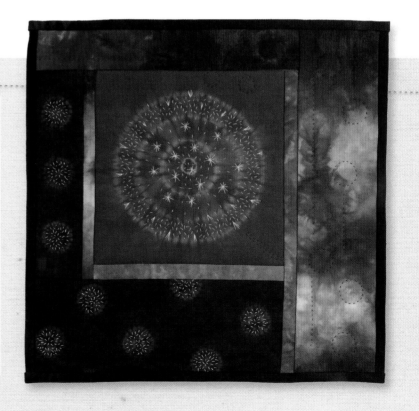

I first worked on a graphic yellow dandelion inspired by one of my photos, but I wasn't happy with the outcome. I unpicked it and replaced the fresh dandelion with a dried one using the first idea I had—to use shibori dyeing to depict the white flower head. I used photos taken in my garden as inspiration for embroidering the textured details. I finally recycled my yellow dandelion in a second quilt.

Françoise JANART

Creating My Piece

needles punches the fibers on the surface down into the bottom fabric, causing them to interlock. I dug through my stash and spent a happy evening playing with the felting attachment, punching different white fibers through green cotton. I loved the result, and knew that I'd found the right technique for my dandelion puffs. The chance to use a brand-new gadget and the result I'd hoped for? I was thrilled.

My felting experiments helped me decide that I wanted to use a hand-dyed fabric with some color variation on it for the background of the piece. I like to dye fabric and indulge in dyeing sprees when the weather is warm. I've never been much good at dyeing fabric with a particular project in mind. (I find that it's like shopping for a particular clothing item when I have a specific need for it—I have a hard time finding it then, but I make great finds when I'm not looking for them!) Instead, I dye fabric to play with color and experiment with different combinations, so I end up with a fabulous assortment of fabrics waiting in my stash until the right project

comes along. I found the perfect piece of fabric that had appealing variations of light and dark green.

With a white chalk pencil, I lightly drew the puff circles and stems to place them where I wanted them. With the wrong side of the green fabric facing up, I needle-felted white silk organza into the green cotton. As I "stitched" with the felting attachment, I was working on the back of my work, pushing the organza fibers through to the front of the green cotton. The more I felted, moving the fabric around in small circles, the denser the white "fluff" became. The resulting white puff was light and wispy, with the

Löwenzahn und Pusteblume

Inspired by all the dandelions that kept popping up via my kids—in their textbooks, craft projects, TV shows, seasonal activities at school, poems, etc.—I strove to make something that had a childlike sensibility. I played off of simple shapes, big stitches, and button details, which are all elements repeatedly found in children's art. Hopefully the subtle surface design and off-center composition keep the piece from looking as if it was actually made by a child.

In an alternate study, I asked myself "What's a very Kristin thing to do?" I thought of the distorted hexagons I'd been using at the time, which reminded me of the traditional Grandmother's Flower Garden quilts with their groups of concentric hexagons. I thought about so many lawns and gardens overrun with dandelions and conceived the title *Grandmother's Flower Garden Is Overrun by Dandelions*. It was my runner-up, made of poufy yellow, lacy white, and leafy green distorted hexagons.

Kristin LaFlamme

semi-transparent effect for which I'd been aiming. Then, using traditional machine stitching and regular thread, I defined the puff circles and the dandelion stems.

At that stage, I layered the top onto cotton batting (I tend to use 80 percent cotton/20 percent polyester batting for most projects), and added a back layer of cotton fabric. I stabilized them with safety pins and used free-motion machine stitching to define some pointy dandelion leaves. Then, with all of the design elements defined, I free-motion quilted soft, curvy lines to create an impression of wind and add texture to the background.

The puffs still needed definition, so using white cotton embroidery floss, I hand-embroidered detail onto

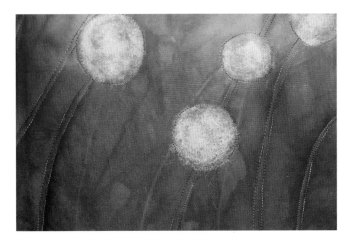

Summer Scourge

Dandelion was our very first theme. I was nervous and therefore wanted to keep it simple. I remember thinking that when we unveiled, everyone would have a close-up of a dandelion. Thankfully this was not the case.

This piece was made using my embellisher so there is no thread involved, only seven needles pushing the fabric into the felt below. I used silk, rayon, nylon, and cotton fabrics. The purple is pieces of fabric I chopped up and sprinkled on the felt. I then covered the whole thing with tulle and "embellished" it.

Karen L. Rip

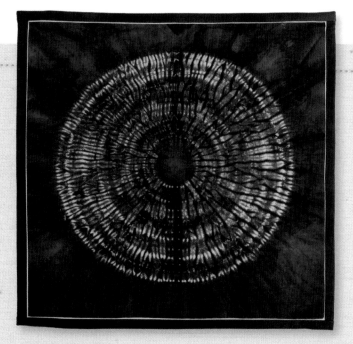

Pièce de Résistance

After a brief, but intense, infatuation with shibori, I once declared that I was "over it" and had made my last piece. Despite this assertion, I was prompted to revisit the shibori-style stitch-resist dyeing technique when it occurred to me that the larch motif would make a splendid dandelion seed head in all its faded glory. Taking this as a lesson in never-say-never, I went on to incorporate shibori techniques in four of my Twelve by Twelve theme works and several of my alternate pieces. This piece is hand-quilted with concentric circles and radiating lines, and finished with a peeper/flange binding.

Brenda Gael Smith

each puff. (Embroidery floss—another box in my closet I knew I'd use again one of these days!) I embroidered some wisps to look as if they'd just flown loose from the puffs. The last layer of embellishment was the most fun. I pulled out my set of pastel crayons. I used dark greens and blues to color shadows, then pale yellow and white to add highlights to the leaves and stems. I highlighted the dandelion puffs with white to make them look softer. Dared I add more? The hardest trick about using pastel crayons, I find, is knowing when to stop. I grabbed one more crayon and added a bit of pale yellow in the center of each puff. There. Done. Put the crayons down and step away. Once I added the narrow quilt binding, my dandelion quilt was finished. Humming the Peter, Paul and Mary song, I titled the piece *Blowin' in the Wind*.

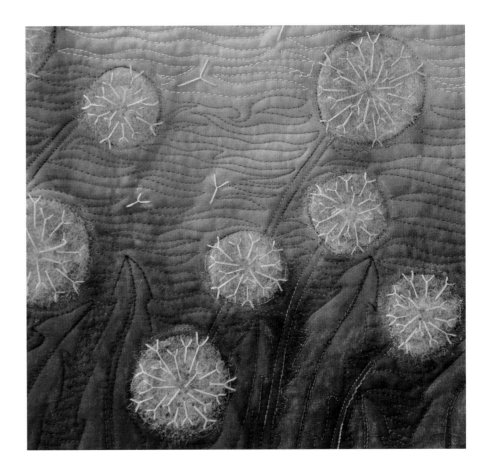

Ferocious Dan

For this first theme, I knew that I had plenty of inspiration right outside in my yard. In my neck of the woods, dandelions are the first burst of color to be seen in the spring and the last in the late fall. I enjoy walking around the yard with my cats and along our walks we see many of these tough little "flowers." I drew and painted my cat directly on a piece of fabric. I then appliquéd this to the quilt background. I created two larger, three-dimensional dandelions with painted Lutradur and added tufts of eyelash yarn for some fluff in the center of the flowers.

Terri Stegmiller

Dandelions in Bloom

I was especially pleased with this challenge result for a number of reasons. I don't always sketch out ideas, and even though my sketches were primitive at best, I was able to work out some ideas that way. I experimented with some different techniques and was able to discover what wouldn't work before I dove into the "real" piece. I ultimately used a technique that was new to me, and even made use of a shiny new gadget. While I often tend to be more graphic in my imagery, I was pleased that I'd stretched a bit into a different direction. I was also able to see the benefit of layering different techniques and materials to add detail and depth.

As we worked toward our first reveal date, we talked about our ideas and approaches to the theme. Many of us searched for dandelion images to inspire us. Brenda and Kristin shared poems about them. Terry made digital drawings, while Françoise showed us the results of her manipulations with photo software. Terri turned to painting, Gerrie to screen-printing. Nikki created a journal of dandelion ideas. While Helen bemoaned her inability to find any trace of dandelions among the brick and concrete of London, the rest of us noticed dandelions—real and illustrated—everywhere.

The results of the challenge were exciting, with a variety of styles and techniques that surprised all of us. I found myself looking at the images again and again, marveling each time at the cleverness and talent in each piece. The Twelve by Twelve challenge was off and running!

Dandelion Wine

Dandelion Wine is a celebration of the color yellow and the joy it embodies. I used everything I could get my hands on. I began by needle-felting six different yarns onto a base fabric. I used embroidery floss to stitch Xs and French knots. I added the beads, brads, buttons, fake flowers, puffs of several other yarns, bits of ribbon, and yellow raffia. I quilted this onto a backing fabric with gold embroidery floss and bound the edges with several yarns. The last touch was the wire swirls and springs. Who said less is more?!

Nikki Wheeler

STARTING YOUR OWN CHALLENGE GROUP

If you wish that you were part of a challenge group, there's a simple solution: Start a group yourself! Here are some tips for starting a challenge group.

What

Figure out what sort of group you want. If you're going to make the effort to form a group, think about the characteristics that will make the group fun and exciting for you. The more you can define the way you'd like the group to be, the more likely you are to end up with a challenge group experience that satisfies you. Also, defining what you want the group to be will help you find group members who want to pursue the same avenues you do. For example:

- Do you want to focus on techniques? General themes?
- Do you want to limit the size of the pieces you make?
- Do you want to focus on art quilting, traditional quilting, or any and all styles?
- Do you prefer to work with more people, or fewer?

Who

Identify who you'd like to be in your group. Ideally, they'll be people whose work inspires you, whose personalities you enjoy, and who will follow through on any commitments the group requires. Maybe you know people in your area that you can meet in person periodically. Perhaps you'd rather not have in-person meetings, but would prefer to use the Internet to connect with people in other places. If you're going to have the group function online, then you'll need people who are comfortable with email, online interaction, and publishing digital photographs.

When

Identify a realistic time frame for your challenges. Allow enough time for challenge periods so that meeting deadlines doesn't become unpleasantly stressful, but be careful not to allow such big gaps that people lose interest.

How

Once you have some ideas about the characteristics of the group you'd want, ask some folks to join you. If you have friends you'd like to play with, invite them. Don't be afraid to invite people you don't know well. Chances are they will be flattered to be invited even if they are unable to participate. Are there members in your quilt guild you wished you knew better? Tell them about your idea. Online, email people whose work you like and ask if they'd be interested in playing with you (and don't be afraid to make images of your work available to them, so they can learn a bit about you.) Most importantly, don't take it personally if people turn you down. People are busy and may not have the time or willingness to focus their creative energies in a challenge group. Keep putting your group ideas out there, and you'll find a few like-minded artists to play with you. Remember, you can have as much fun with one other person as with 11. Last, consider starting small (with two or three rounds, or a relatively short time commitment), and then assess whether to go further at that point.

—Diane Perin Hock

Theme 2: **Chocolate**

chosen by: **Françoise Jamart**

I chose this word simply because I love good chocolate so much. I think almost everyone, especially every woman, has an emotional relationship with it. And of course I'm convinced that Belgian chocolate is the best!

Obviously Chocolate

Chocolate Love

Unsuitable Things

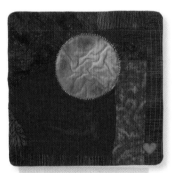
Soft Centre

Cacao y Canela

Still Life Without Chocolate

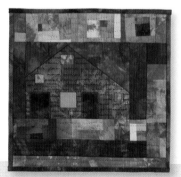
Love, Chocolate and Patchwork

The Marquise de Coëtlogon

Cocoa Beans

Organic Chocolate (Dark)

Choco Latte

Chocolate Desire

Chocolate Desire

Nikki Wheeler

The loving, encouraging nature of the group has allowed me to step out of my comfort zone and try so many new things. I know that my work will be gladly accepted and highlighted among this group of friends.

Nikki Wheeler

A New Beginning

I often wonder how I ended up so lucky, in such a wonderful group filled with amazing women on such a grand adventure. When Diane invited me to join her in this online group I couldn't believe that I was included with all these accomplished art quilters. I can't tell you how inadequate I felt towards the task. How could I measure up? I had only discovered the joys of art quilting and fiber art six months before and had barely started blogging. I definitely didn't think anyone had really noticed me, a mom with four young children, desperately trying to carve out a little sanity in her crazy world. Despite my insecurities, I couldn't pass up this opportunity. I had no idea what I was getting into, but I knew it

would be good. I was being offered a chance to be a part of something— to belong.

My art quilting adventure began with a much-needed afternoon escape from all my motherly obligations. Thankfully, Dad took over and I headed out to the Barnes & Noble magazine racks. I looked past all the parenting, homeschooling, and even gardening magazines to the craft section. I was looking for something I love, something that was just for me, some way to regain the me that had been lost with the years of babies. And what did I find? *Quilting Arts, Cloth Paper Scissors, Somerset Studio*. I discovered the world of art quilting and mixed media. The doors opened and I gladly stepped

Obviously Chocolate

I love chocolate, so it was no trouble enjoying a few sweet treats so I would have shiny wrappers to incorporate in my quilt. This is a wonky interpretation of a box of chocolates. I used sheer organza and cheesecloth for a sense of layers. The variety of browns remind me of milk, dark, and white chocolate. The candy wrappers were surprisingly easy to incorporate. I carefully cleaned them, added fusible webbing, and mixed them in with the fabrics. The swirly free-motion quilting mimics the designs on the top of chocolate truffles.

Deborah Boschert

through. My life hasn't been the same since. I started creating and my soul bloomed. The next step in the process was to jump on the Internet and start exploring. Wow! The world of blogging and all its bounty. I was a little nervous about starting my own blog. I didn't know if anyone would really be interested in my creations. I didn't feel comfortable calling myself an artist. I blogged for a couple months before I told anybody about my online presence. Eventually, I joined Diane's Artful Quilters Web Ring. Although nervous, I wanted to share myself with others and get feedback. Thankfully, everyone was very nice and encouraging. I admit negative feedback would have crushed me. I

am so glad that I was willing to take that risk. Because of it, Diane saw my work and was willing to take a chance in inviting me to join what soon became Twelve by Twelve. I am so honored to be a Twelve.

Twelve by Twelve has offered me an excuse to play and explore with art quilts. My commitment to the group has allowed me to set aside time from my obligations as wife and mother to create. My family understands that I have "work" to do and have become used to the bimonthly deadlines. I have used each of my Twelve by Twelve quilts to experiment and try different techniques. I've explored various construction and embellishment techniques, including my encrusted *Dandelion*

Wine (page 22), painted *Illumination Celebration* (page 77), fused *Transcendental Curve* (page 104), hand-stitched *Mom's Hideout* (page 118), and raw-edge appliqué on *Simply ME* (page 146). The loving, encouraging nature of the group has allowed me to step out of my comfort zone and try so many new things. I know that my work will be gladly accepted and highlighted among this group of friends. These amazing women have become important friends who encourage me and often offer laughs and perspective completely separate from quilting. I am encouraged artistically, spiritually, and relationally.

Chocolate Love

Or, "What happens to chocolate when it comes into my house!" Valentine chocolate was the inspiration for this piece. I made a scan of shibori fabric and gave it a creamy chocolate color change. I printed the image on silk charmeuse. The other elements were created from photos of Valentine candies and real kisses that were printed on organza. Thermofax screens were used to print the words with paint. The fabric elements are fused in place. The piece was completed with simple quilting lines.

Exploring the Theme

Appropriately, Françoise chose Chocolate for our second challenge. What a fun concept to explore! I think it may have been one of the favorite themes to research. We discovered so many different flavors and forms. Kristin brought us a wide selection of chocolates available at the German Christmas Markets and a tour of the chocolate museum in Köln, Germany. Deborah pointed out the captivating Hershey's-inspired fashions created on *Project Runway*. Helen tried to convince us all to share in her madness with a Cadbury Roses jingle stuck in our heads. Beautiful, chocolate-covered strawberries were shared by Terri. Brenda incorporated chocolate research into her San Francisco travels. Gerrie reminded us of Forrest Gump's famous line, "Life was like a box of chocolates: You never know what you're gonna get." Kirsten brought us the "bush flavors" of Brisbane chocolatier Peter Mayfield, including Kakudu plum, wattleseed, lemon myrtle, and eucalyptus. Definitely nothing this American girl has ever tried. I would be interested, though, in trying another Australian tradition Kirsten shared with us—the Chocolate Orgasm—featuring Tim Tams and hot coffee. Chocolate and bacon, discovered by Deborah, might have been one of the strangest. I can't tell you if it is actually good or not, because nobody was brave enough to try it. The strangest presentation was probably the chocolate sushi that included white-chocolate crab sticks and octopus, strawberry-flavored chocolate tuna fillet, and apricot-flavored Gummi eggs, all wrapped in dark chocolate. Michael Recchiuti, owner of Recchiuti Confections, even commented on our blog when I posted about his cookbook, *Chocolate Obsession*. Needless to say, this was a theme we could all gladly relate to.

Unsuitable Things

Mulling over associations with the word "chocolate," I was reminded of my old school biology teacher who frequently used the phrase, "as useful as a chocolate teapot." That in turn reminded me of one of the lists in *The Pillow Book of Sei Shonagon*, that of "Unsuitable Things." I typed up that copyright-free list in a handwriting font and printed it on fabric, then manipulated a photo of a teapot so it appeared to be melting and added it on top. I used commercial fabric with calligraphy for the border.

Helen M Conway

Creating My Piece

Despite all the interesting varieties of chocolate, I decided to go with a more straightforward approach to the theme. I used a box of chocolates to capture the sensual joy of a delicious candy melting in one's mouth. Bacon, lavender, or sushi weren't allowed to interfere with my simple yet sophisticated pleasure.

I've never been one to follow the "rules" when it comes to creating. I just can't do it the way everyone else does. Some of it may stem from my fears that I just won't be able to do it as well as those who have come before. I often don't try something unless I know I will succeed. So I try something completely different that I have never seen before. And that

Soft Centre

The magical work of Jude Hill (www.spiritcloth. typepad.com) intrigues me and makes my fingers ache to stitch. It took weeks of thinking about chocolate before a small piece of velvet presented itself from my scrap basket and merged in my mind with Jude's free stitching. I pieced an abstract background of chocolate and hand-painted the velvet with dyes that matched the colors of fruit fondant centers. The circle of velvet is reverse appliquéd and then caught with small hand-sewn stitches to make a rumpled soft center.

Kirsten Duncan

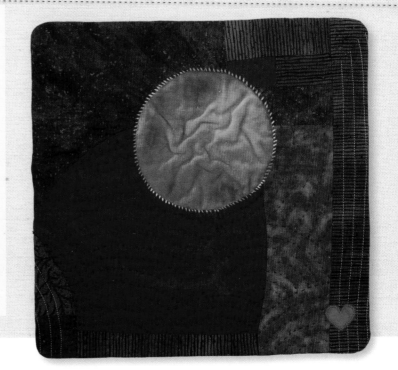

is how I first approached quilting. No traditional piecing, appliqué, or even painting. I instead opted for the backwards approach. I started with plain white muslin, added batting and backing fabric, and started quilting. I love the texture of densely quilted lines and the richness of a sketchy line. I quilted the fabric with white thread using dense swirls and overlapping lines. For the darkest values of chocolate, I used a piece of black fabric and black thread. I then washed the fabric in hot water to soften the fabric, puff up the ridges, and deepen the valleys.

Painting came next in the process. I used three large pieces of quilted fabric to create light, medium, and dark values. I added various shades of brown paint to create different

Cacao y Canela

Cacao y Canela (chocolate and cinnamon) was the drink of the Aztecs and Mayans and is the sweet perfume of Oaxaca. The "chocolate" theme gave me an excuse to indulge my love of Mexican Talavera pottery. The mug is my own design, using elements of several different Talavera pieces that I own. And the background tile is based on the tile we had just had laid in our new house. It was great fun to put this piece all together!

Terry Grant

flavors and intensities of chocolate. I used watered-down acrylic, fabric, and craft paints. I love the different effects caused by the way the watery paint dries on the quilted fabric. The color tends to rise to the ridges of fabric as the water evaporates. The thread also traps the pigment, but typically the valley sides are left a lighter value. I also added more concentrated paint to deepen the colors and add variety, especially to the medium and dark values. I had to use additional dry-brush techniques to change the black fabric to brown. Overcoming my negative bias, I stretched my limited vision of brown and explored the different hues, tints, tones, and values. Some appeared a little red, others coppery or gray. Individually they didn't

Still Life Without Chocolate

Chocolate is a treasured part of my daily life, so I was delighted when Françoise announced this theme choice. After photographing and sketching cupcakes and cake slices, I realized that the most appropriate depiction of my relationship with chocolate would to be to illustrate it just having been eaten. Chocolate doesn't sit around for long in my house! I studied candy wrappers, which meant that as a dedicated researcher, I had to empty a variety of them. I liked the look of a particular wrapper with its shiny foil and brown pleated paper. To create them with fabric, I fused fabric shapes, machine-stitched them, and added detail and highlights with fabric paint and pastel crayons.

Diane Perin Hock

necessarily say chocolate, but together they created a rich and varied flavor, much like the varieties of chocolate we all discovered through our research.

When the paint dried, I started cutting up the fabrics into ½-inch-wide (1.3 cm) strips and 1- to 2-inch (2.5- to 5.1-cm) squares. I then sewed the strips around the squares in a simple log cabin style, using a dense zigzag stitch to attach the butted edges. At this point I started the design process of laying out the quilt. I tried to vary the placement of the large and medium squares and balanced the light, medium, and dark values throughout the piece. I tried to separate similar values, but

Love, Chocolate and Patchwork

This is my house. It's full of love, chocolate, and patchwork. As I wrote down every word I associated with chocolate, it soon became clear that many of these words, feelings, facts, things, were related to my family, to my children, and therefore to my home too. I wrote the most meaningful words on a home-dyed chocolate brown fabric. This would be the house. I used log cabin blocks to construct the borders of the quilt.

Françoise JANART

found that it just wasn't possible with the combination of shades and sizes of the squares. When I finished laying out the outlined squares, I filled in the gaps with simple 1-inch squares.

At this point the puzzle became the order in which I needed to piece the quilt together, once again with a dense zigzag stitch. My goal was to stitch in simple straight lines, without having to fit a piece into a corner, but I had to make a few direction changes with this design. Looking at it now, I can see a few of the basic building blocks. Perhaps you can explore the quilt and determine the best stitching order to minimize direction changes.

The Marquise de Coëtlogon

My inspiration was an excerpt from a seventeenth-century letter at the Chocolate Museum in Köln, Germany. Writer Madame de Sévigné advised her then-pregnant daughter that she not consume chocolate lest she, like the chocoholic Marquise de Coëtlogon, give birth to a cocoa-colored child. The story seemed outlandish to our modern sensibilities, yet I was intrigued by it, and the unconventional take on chocolate it offered. Incorporating our chosen medium of fabric, I expressed the story visually as a cross between the erotic frivolity of a Fragonard painting and the improvisation and patterning of a slave "story quilt."

Kristin LaFlamme

To finish the edges of the quilt, I didn't want a traditional binding (how could you guess?). A plain strip of fabric just wouldn't work with this highly textured quilt. So I incorporated copper tape, traditionally used for a soldering base. The tape is sticky, so I just needed to wrap it around the edge of the quilt. I folded it in half before removing the paper backing and then slipped the edge of the quilt into the fold.

Throughout the process I was worried that the quilt wouldn't quite say "chocolate" with all the sensuality I wanted. As a mom with small children and little adult adventure, chocolate is my guilty pleasure, my little bit of euphoria within the chaos of family life. It is filled with such feeling and emotion. How to capture that moment of bliss when, in the midst of all the craziness of life, one takes a bite of a really good chocolate truffle? The sweet ooze melting in one's mouth and washing all the stress away for a second? In the end, I asked my daughter what the quilt made her think of and she answered, "Those chocolates that we had the sample of at Costco that I really want." If the quilt says, "Lindt truffles," then I must have captured what I was after.

On Reveal Day, I am always amazed at the diversity of the quilts within every theme. The richness and complexity blows me away. Deborah and I both depicted boxes, but our techniques were completely different. Brenda, Kirsten, and Diane each chose individual chocolates. Brenda used her wonderful, wonky piecing to create the lines in a large tablet of chocolate. Kirsten used soft

Cocoa Beans

The Chocolate theme suggested brown, which I really wanted to avoid. Trying to be a little untraditional, I went right to the source of the subject, the cocoa bean, which goes through a number of color changes while maturing. I used hand-dyed cotton/silk blend for all the fabrics, couched some yarn around the edge of each one, and then did some hand stitching to finish it off.

Karen L. Rip

velvet and hand stitching to depict a fruity soft center. Diane instead chose the opposite approach and gave us an empty wrapper, alluding to a just-eaten peanut butter cup. Terry and Terri both gave us liquid chocolate. Terry created her beautiful *Cacao y Canela* with fabric appliqué, while Terri painted a pleasing morning scene with an inviting mocha, chocolate treats, and sunny flowers. Françoise created a warm, inviting home with chocolate walls surrounding her loving family. Gerrie explored the more sensual aspects of chocolate. Helen introduced us to the phrase, "useless as a chocolate teapot." And Kristin, Kristin upped the ante for us all on future challenges with her amazing *The Marquise de Coëtlogon*. Her unique take on the subject and amazing attention to detail once again reinforced the idea that I'm out of my league.

Where I Create

My studio space is starting to take over the house—a foolish idea, considering we have six people, who each have plenty of toys and hobbies, living in 1,300 square feet. I do technically have a "studio" in one bay of our detached garage, converted by the previous owner, but I never could find the time to make it out there. I would be crazy if I left the four kids in the house unsupervised. Instead I have planted myself firmly in the middle of our living space. I am able to create and still be with the family. I can participate in the conversations and be available for all the things moms need to be available for. My kids have learned that art and creating are just part of normal life and not something that needs a special space or time.

In the beginning, I just used the dining room table and stored my supplies on a shelf. For painting,

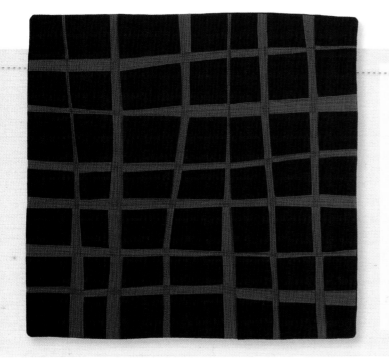

Organic Chocolate (Dark)

Chocolate is near and dear to my heart. Upon hearing about this theme, I was immediately inspired by the lines in the large tablets of chocolate that often make their way into my grocery basket. This "dark chocolate" piece is part of a trio of chocolate quilts—dark, milk, and white. It was created using freeform cutting and piecing from commercial fabrics and machine quilted with whole-cloth facing finish.

Brenda Gael Smith

I had a sheet of plexiglass that I placed on the table, kitchen counter, and even occasionally over the sink filled with dirty dishes. My sewing machine would be set up and taken down between meals or we would eat picnic style on the floor if I was busy working on something. I quickly filled the bookshelves in the living room and added a china cabinet, not for dishes, but for ribbons, yarns, felt, and other supplies. The throw blankets were kicked out of the cabinets under the window seat and in moved my paints and fabrics. Finally I moved the couch and added a desk for my sewing machine in the living room. My family has learned to watch movies or play video games over the whir of the machine. I added white decorative boxes to hold the overflowing creations.

I never quite know what crazy thing I am going to want to add to a quilt, so I make sure to have plenty of choices on hand. I have boxes of beads, buttons, hardware store finds, wires, and scrapbooking supplies. Trims, ribbons, and yarns are overflowing. Plus I have discovered a love of hand-spun yarn and hand-dyed wool felt. I always try to add a little something to my quilts to make them uniquely mine. The only problem is that I'm starting to see more and more of my things without a home. They are stacking up on the side of the desk and sitting in brown packing boxes. For some reason, when everything gets put away I must think it is time to buy more. For now I will just blame it on my dad and his Boy Scout training—always be prepared!

Choco Latte

Chocolate, dark chocolate to be precise, is certainly one of the many wonders of the world. I love the look of opening a box of fancy chocolates and how they are all perfectly formed and shaped with little swirls of decoration. That was my inspiration for part of this quilt. The other was my love of mocha lattes. I combined the two into an inviting scene by painting the plate of chocolates, the latte, and the flowers directly onto the fabric background. If you look close, you'll see the words "choco" and "latte" printed on the fabric.

Terri Stegmiller

CREATING TIME AND SPACE FOR ART

All 12 of us struggle to find time in our lives for creativity, and not all of us are lucky enough to have dedicated studios. Maybe you're in that situation too. Here are our thoughts about how to make room in your day and your home for creativity:

Have a dedicated table where you can leave your sewing machine set up. Having your machine out and ready for use will make you more likely to spend a few minutes sewing.

Create a separate art area in a spare bedroom, basement, garage, garden shed, or unused formal dining or living room. You can spread out, be messy, and projects don't need to be cleaned up at the end of the day.

Create an art space within your family living space. Add a table or desk in a corner of the kitchen or family room. You can create and still be readily available for your family.

If you have school-age children, have a homework space adjacent to your creative space. They can work at a desk while you are at your machine nearby. You can help with homework, keep them company, and work on a project at the same time.

Save time by creating near the kitchen. You can easily do a little creating while your food is cooking. Using a slow-cooker and cooking freezer meals ahead of time can free up additional time.

Create an "on-the-go" art kit. Have a sketchbook and drawing supplies or straightforward handwork ready in a fun bag that is easy to grab as you're heading out.

If you have toddlers, use a sewing machine with an on/off button so you can unplug the foot pedal while they are underfoot.

Pack up that china and crystal you rarely use, and fill the china cabinet with colorful fabric, ribbons, and threads.

Use decorative boxes or baskets to store your supplies "in sight."

Keep individual projects on a cookie sheet, in a clean, flat pizza box, or in a similar low-profile container. Threads, fabrics, and embellishments won't slide off and they can be stored on a shelf or even the top of the kitchen cabinets.

Hire cleaning help if possible. Schedule a dedicated cleaning time once a week and don't let it creep into art time. Set the timer and clean for 30 minutes, then reward yourself with 30 minutes of art time. If all else fails, ignore the dust and clutter!

Schedule personal creative time. Put it on your calendar and honor it like any other appointment. Don't answer the phone or emails during this time.

Schedule creative play dates and parties with friends instead of lunch or coffee.

Don't over-commit yourself. Allow free time to just explore.

Pay attention to the mindless ways you use time. Limit your time playing computer games, roaming the Internet, or chatting on Facebook, and dedicate the balance of that time to working on art.

Join an art swap, collaborative project, or critique group to provide accountability and deadlines. If a deadline makes you work better, then find ways of creating deadlines to keep you creating.

Create a blog to inspire you to create so you have pictures to post. Be fed by the positive comments and online friendships.

Have several projects going at once so you can work on whichever stage best fits the moment.

Train your family and friends that art is important. Working on art is "work" and needs to be honored as such.

Have fun and set the joy of creativity as a priority.

—Nikki Wheeler

Theme 3: Community

I chose Community. In my own work, I was transitioning from mostly landscapes to focusing on villages and homes with roots. I figured if I was choosing the theme, I could pick something that would further my personal work at the same time!

Attached Disconnected

Birds of a Feather

District Six

Brunswick Street

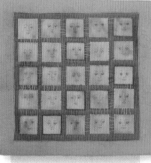

Ties that Bind

All Together Now

Neighbourhood

Community

Similar Differences

My People

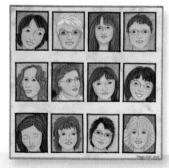

12 by 12 Community

Fiber Art Community, By the Inch

Brunswick Street

Kirsten Duncan

I adore the intensity of color, the rich and unexpected patterns that emerge when I cut the yardage into small pieces, the depth and layers that build as I put them back together. Most of all, I enjoy the accidental quality of it all—as Brenda says, "The serendipity!"

Kirsten Duncan

A New Community

The phenomenon of Internet communities is a fascinating one. Although I had been aware of chat rooms and vaguely knew what a blog was, it wasn't until I moved from New Zealand to a remote Outback town in Australia and slid into an artistic funk that I began to regularly read blogs. In February 2006 I started my own blog. My first post included this quote from my teenaged son, Clancy, "What on earth do you want a blog for? You don't do anything except make quilts!" I hope that what he meant was, "What will you write about and who will read it?" Isn't that the question every blogger asks herself? The answer was very quickly made clear: write about quilts and quilters will read it. I have been teaching quiltmaking for many years now and I had noticed that there is a very high rate of computer use among quilters. What I didn't know was how many quilting bloggers there are—I soon found out! Early on, I joined a "blog ring," a group of blogs with a common thread who all link to each other. It happened to be Diane's Artful Quilters blog ring.

And then Diane sent me the invitation to participate in her Good Idea. I was sorely missing the inspiring company of my old quilting friends in New Zealand and so I quickly said yes (all the while thinking, "Maybe she's confused me with someone else? She wants me to join a group with Terry Grant in it?!"). The discipline of a commitment to 11 other people was just what I needed to

Attached Disconnected

As I pondered the community theme, it was difficult for me to find an angle to explore in fabric. Ultimately, I decided to symbolize the feeling of being a part of a group by circumstance, like a neighborhood, job, or church, and yet not feeling completely connected with the group in spirit, attitude, or lifestyle. The embellishments are items that might connect things: a safety pin, a key, a button. This feeling can be uncomfortable and I don't think I expressed it very well in this quilt. It's my least favorite of my collection, but that discomfort is part of the larger experience. It's an important part of the process.

Deborah Boschert

make myself produce new work. I immediately promised myself that this Twelve by Twelve project was going to be fun. I wouldn't try to impress anyone or make perfect quilts; I would just enjoy the whole thing and maybe try some new techniques. That was it. No rules. Best of all, I had a new quilt group.

And a New Challenge

It doesn't take very long at all for online relationships to flourish and we quickly found that our group was much like any quilting group anywhere. Each member's worries and joys and daily tangles become part of the group's thoughts. So when Kristin announced Community as our third theme we were, as she said

in her blog announcement, already "...forming a nice little community here...." Indeed, we were! We thought about each other all the time...

Françoise—I wonder what you guys are doing now. Are you thinking and working hard on your 12 x 12 quilts? I'm very curious....

We communicated sometimes daily, sometimes weekly, sometimes less. But we were thinking about the same issues, the same ideas. Each announcement of a new theme was generating these responses: some knew immediately what their quilt would be like, some had ten thousand ideas and just had to chase down the right one, and others did a little wing-flapping and squawking for a while! On a couple

of occasions I was like a deer in the headlights.

Terri—At first I thought this theme would be very challenging for me and that I'd be struggling....But...I am very much enjoying being a part of this community. I am going to create my "community" quilt based on all of the 12 x 12 members.

Brenda—Work on my community-themed quilt has stalled due to being unexpectedly stranded in Sydney for nearly three days with car troubles.

Nikki—I was really surprised at how hard this challenge has been. I was plagued by distractions and other obligations, along with inspiration that I just didn't have the skill to carry out.

Birds of a Feather

A community means that the members have something in common—where they live, a religion, shared genetics, hobbies, or a workplace. I thought birds hanging out together was a great metaphor for community. I couldn't decide whether I wanted city birds or country birds. You can see where I went—I had fun abstracting the city architecture, using my stash of commercial fabrics. The fabric elements are fused and quilted.

Gerrie Congdon

Let Me Think About That

My family's move to the Outback was just one of many that we have made over the 27 years that Peter and I have been married. We've been doomed to our international marriage and thus spend our days traveling and moving between two countries—he is an Australian, I am a New Zealander. As such, we have changed our residence fairly frequently and I have had many reasons to consider the concept of community at length and in depth. We have lived in cities and regional towns and very small rural towns. We even lived in a farmhouse for a time (oh, heaven!).

Not long before this theme was announced, I traveled to Melbourne to teach at a large quilting convention. In a few hours of spare time, I went to Brunswick Street, in Fitzroy. This inner-city neighborhood is my favorite part of Melbourne. It effervesces with life and art. As I sat in a small restaurant with a couple of friends, I watched the people going past. I saw a man who looked just like Robert Winston ride past on an ancient bicycle, as well as teenagers who had styled themselves after Japan's Harajuku girls, couples of every variety imaginable, a

middle-aged transsexual in an extraordinary blonde beehive wig. I thought to myself—this is community! This is wonderful! There is a place for everyone here. It doesn't matter who you are, whether you want an audience or anonymity, there is a place for you. Well, that was probably just a daydream. I'm sure that nirvana doesn't really exist, but when Kristin told us our new theme, I knew that I wanted my quilt to represent that place.

District Six

I have a great love for South Africa and this theme made me recall my visit to District Six in Cape Town. This was a vibrant, multi-ethnic community that was cleared during the apartheid era. Over 60,000 occupants were forced to move to the "homelands" where there was little or no infrastructure or employment, or else ended up in desolate "townships" in the Cape Flats. The area was destined for redevelopment, but in fact was never built on again save for a token number of new houses that were "returned" to a handful of old residents. I stamped the words District Six and used photos of the old street-name signs, now on display at the District Six Museum, to create a frame. I machine-embroidered small houses on Pelmet Vilene (a type of interfacing not sold in the U.S.), and hung them like mobiles to represent both the inadequacy of the recent measures to repopulate and the hole remaining in the community.

Helen M Conway

And So, to the Cloth

I decided on a simple tree covered in leaves of all colors. The tree, with its strong branches and common roots, holds together and supports all of the leaves that, in this case, are free to flourish and be whatever they are. A cliché? Maybe, but one that is near to my heart. I have long had a love of tree-of-life designs, and leaf shapes recur in many things that I make. I have cut thousands of leaves from cloth, usually freehand with scissors. I often use a concertina fold to cut as many as eight at a time. I enjoy the variation in shape and size achieved by cutting this way, although lately I have been using leaves cut for me by my sister with her laser cutter.

Ties that Bind

Community is a very abstract idea to capture graphically. First I lined up my little faces in an organized grid but it seemed that organization wasn't enough. The group becomes a community only when connections are made. I was at a retreat with fellow Twelve, Gerrie, and she had some hand-dyed floss in exactly the colors I was working with. I knew it was just what I needed to make the connections between the individuals in my community. Of course she was ready to share—that's what community is about!

Terry Grant

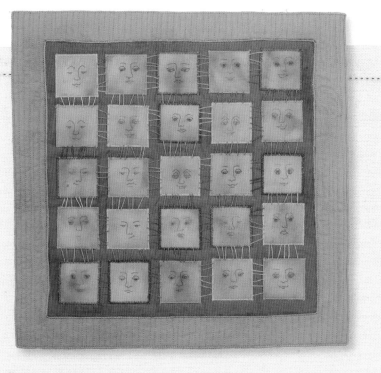

My appliqué shapes are always backed with fusible webbing and machine stitched. Fusible webbing has been a good friend to me for many years now. I love the immediacy of it, the ease with which I can quickly create—sometimes making a design that I have been working on in my head for a long time and other times using a collage process that evolves organically.

Most of the Twelves choose at times to create their own fabrics. Among the Twelve by Twelve quilt collection are many examples of dyeing, over-painting, printing, stamping—all manner of fabric creation and modification. However, my love is commercially printed fabric; on these pages are a few examples of pieces done with a variety of prints.

All Together Now

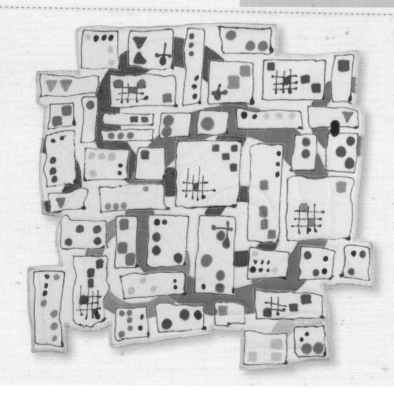

This theme and this project gave me the most difficulty of all of the challenges. I tend to think in a literal way, but I knew that I wanted to push myself toward a more abstract depiction of "community." When I thought about characteristics of community, I was struck by the sense of disparate things forming a whole. I thought of words like "unity," "messiness," "cohesion," "jumble," "interlocking," and I contemplated the sense of things fitting or not fitting together. This colorful and chaotic piece resulted. It is a whole-cloth piece, painted and machine stitched. The irregular edges, atypical for me, seemed to suit my depiction of this theme.

Diane Perin Hock

I adore the intensity of color, the rich and unexpected patterns that emerge when I cut the yardage into small pieces, the depth and layers that build as I put them back together. Most of all, I enjoy the accidental quality of it all—as Brenda says, "The serendipity!" For example, the background fabric of *Brunswick Street* comes from a shirt that I bought at thrift shop. I was attracted to the colors and the wonderful, swirling design that reminds me of wind moving through the tree. After the tree was finished and there was an area of background that needed quilting, it was logical to follow the lines of the printed pattern. I used an amazing variegated thread that adds yet more color, sings out, "Follow me!" and sends your eye floating across the quilt with the wind. The regularity of the design provides a calming and steadying foil against the chaotic quality of the appliqué. If I had created the background fabric, I doubt I would have considered making a pattern such as this.

The fabric choices for the leaves were easy. I knew they would be all different colors and patterns, so variety was the key here. The tree itself needed to be strong enough to hold its own against the busyness of the rest and as I trawled through my scrap box, there appeared this mustard piece. I have a love/hate thing

Neighbourhood

Nice little houses with small gardens...this is my lovely, quiet, and friendly neighborhood. But as our children are growing, the links between our families seem to be fading. I sometimes see each house as a kind of spiral centering on itself. Don't get me wrong, I still like the place where I live, but I'm a bit nostalgic for the good old times when the kids were all playing together in the street.

Françoise JANART

decorated it. How do I describe the pleasure it gives me to arrange fragments of color and pattern this way? It is blissful. It must fire very special synapses in my brain!

Initially I was going to put only leaves on the tree. In my head I saw hundreds of them! However the small format squashed that idea (hmm...maybe I need to make a big one?) and so there are not as many as I envisioned. But I did add some rather crazy and cheap-looking flowers, fruits, and nuts! We all have those in our communities, don't we?

The moment when the quilt reveals itself to me is always the best part of quiltmaking. I have to admit that after that it's just a hard slog until it's finished (usually). The technical requirement of stitching it all down is the aspect that I least enjoy. Having said that, there are

with the color mustard. Of itself, I find it a very unpleasant color but as a side-by-side companion with other colors it can do wonderful things. Put it alongside jacaranda blue or lavender and it makes my heart skip a beat!

This particular piece of mustard cloth had a bonus; it was sprinkled with glitter. It's like an ugly stepsister dressed for the prince's ball. So, I ironed fusible web to the back of it and free-hand cut a tree. A basic tree. Nothing special. And then I

Community

Expressing the feeling of being in a community without actually belonging to it was a difficult abstraction for me, but one that I wanted to accomplish with this piece. The quilt is literally woven out of the fabric of my community: shopping bags with drawings of the homes in my neighborhood traced onto them. I cut and pieced an X through the woven square to create a barrier or window separating the viewer (me) from the scene.

Kristin LaFlamme

many times when the quilting and surface decoration are essential parts of capturing the vision. But once that vision is realized? I have to discipline myself to see it through to completion.

I had intended to satin-stitch or blanket-stitch around each leaf—which are the techniques I most often use—but these little leaves would have been overwhelmed by either method. Instead a lighter touch was needed, so I free-motion stitched around the tree several times and sewed a few veins onto each leaf. I like the pen-and-ink effect of the black thread over the bright colors of the leaves.

This quilt happened quickly and, yes, effortlessly. It is not a perfect quilt, and it is not a prizewinner. If I made it again, no doubt I would fret over the details, discard the tawdry flowers and cheap buttons. But I love this little quilt. It still sings to my soul.

Similar Differences

I was stretched for this challenge. Being a somewhat literal person, I wanted to try something abstract. There are both positive and negative aspects of belonging to a community: the feeling of being in the right place and the feeling of being left out, or on the fringe. This was made using fused sheers, screen-printing, and hand stitching.

Karen L. Rip

Twelve Different Directions?

The Twelves' exploration of Community found a broad range of expression.

Kristin, having chosen to capture "the feeling of being in a community without actually belonging to it," also admitted, "You'd think that since this theme was my idea, it would have been easy, but you'd be wrong." Her complex idea resulted in an equally complex quilt with much to look at and consider.

Terri followed through with her plan to celebrate the Twelves, and her portrait of our group thrilled (and flattered!) us all, while also encouraging us to contemplate the meaning of our relationships with each other.

Although Diane expressed doubt as to the success of her quilt, the rest of us were sure that she had successfully and beautifully conveyed the order and disorder of communities. She and Karen recognized similar themes in one another's quilts and both chose abstract imagery. Karen was not the first—nor the last—Twelve to feel stretched during the making of her quilt, and I think for all of us that has been a rewarding aspect of the Twelve by Twelve project.

Most of us have other Internet connections as well as this project, and Nikki drew upon her collection of "inchies" acquired from other online quilters to make her quilt. A true community quilt!

Every one of Helen's quilts is a teaching tool and every detail has meaning. *District Six* made us think about a community further from home, a community in need of our thought.

Brenda made *My People* and at first glance it appears to be very simple. As we considered this stack of cutout humans, however, we each attributed different circumstances to the figures. Likewise, in *Neighbourhood*, made by Françoise, we all saw meaning in the beautifully stitched and elegant shapes. How emotive a simple image can be!

Several of the quilts worked with a grid format, including both Deborah's *Attached Disconnected* and Terry's *Ties that Bind*, but more surprising was the obvious similarity between the Xs that transect both Gerrie's *Birds of a Feather* and Kristin's *Community*.

My People

Originally conceived as a series of interconnected, cut-out paper doll stencils, my "people" took on a life of their own as handpainted stamps. Some defied definition and assumed certain imperfections. Others lost their grip and can be seen flailing and teetering despite being surrounded by people. A community can be like that. This piece was stamped with fabric paints using a foam cutout then machine quilted.

Brenda Gael Smith

A Home for My Making

In each of the homes we have had over the years there has always been a corner somewhere that was full of my Sewing Stuff. Unfortunately for my family, sometimes that corner has been our dining table! We have had periods of "gulp" months when the table was perpetually buried by projects and fabric and the sewing machine. In other houses, I have had a sewing room of my own. The most indulgent was a room that had once been a double garage. It was huge, with a potbelly woodstove and sofas. I filled it.

A few years ago we left the Outback and moved to large coastal town. We now live in a very small townhouse, and all were greatly relieved when I opened a small quilting and craft shop in August 2009. Now my sewing stuff lives at the shop and I do everything there but a little hand sewing, which sometimes comes home with me in the evenings. This little corner of the classroom is mine and I have here useful materials and also things that I find beautiful. I have two sewing machines that I use regularly. My workhorse is a high-end electronic embroidery machine but I enjoy the romance of a antique lightweight machine, too.

Inspiration is never far away. Nothing thrills me more than color, and beautiful or unexpected combinations are a joy to me. I spend time almost every day online looking at Flickr, reading blogs, and viewing the work of all kinds of artists and designers. Books and magazines have supported a lifetime of self-directed learning.

12 by 12 Community

I was still finding it hard to believe I was a part of this fabulous group when we learned about this theme. I belonged to a wonderful group of 12 artists making 12-inch (30.5-cm) quilts—a 12 by 12 community. I started sketching the faces of each member, using the photos that we had posted on the blog. Once I had created 12 faces I was happy with, I then traced them onto 12 pieces of fabric. I painted each face and then appliquéd them to the quilt background. I like to think this is how we would all look if we were cartoon characters.

Terri Stegmiller

Learning from the Twelves

For me, an interesting benefit of involvement in this project has been a greater understanding of my design processes. As a champion procrastinator, I would castigate myself constantly for delaying the physical process of making a quilt until the last minute.

I now recognize the enormous amount of thought I give to projects before I begin the construction and how valuable that stage is. Many ideas are considered and culled, techniques for construction critiqued and planned. In part, my new understanding of myself has come about through Gerrie's descriptions of her process and also comments from the other Twelves, like this one from Diane:

...after much lying around on the couch in front of the fireplace to do vigorous thinking, I landed on something I am eager to explore.

The true blessing of this is that now I'm kinder to myself about other things, too.

Fiber Art Community, By the Inch

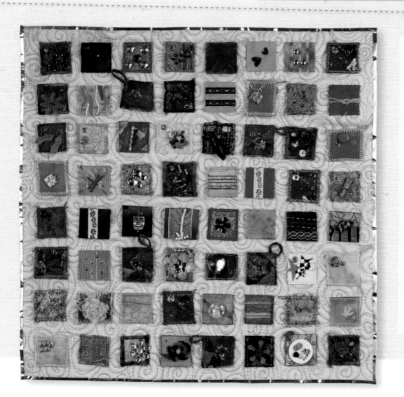

My quilt was inspired by the wonderful online fiber art community. I used the inchies I received from a FiberArtBits swap. Each represents a member of the community and the valuable contribution she brings. I quilted the silver painted fabric with gold metallic thread. The swirling, spiraling quilting lines are for the chaos of each of our lives, while the grid is the touch of structure that ties our lives together, our passion for fiber art.

Nikki Wheeler

FINDING INSPIRATION ONLINE

I have never paid quite so much attention to chairs as I did in December 2008 and January 2009. Office chairs, the seats in our car, park benches—every place to rest one's rump became infinitely fascinating after Deborah announced our new theme as Chairs.

As rich as the stimulus of the Real World can be, we Twelves meet and work on the Internet and it seems only natural, therefore, that we would also seek inspiration there. This wonderland of images and thoughts is an easy one in which to get completely lost. At times, I have been overwhelmed by the volume of information that presents after one brief inquiry—just type the word "chair" into any search engine and see how many images appear. I got 101,000,000 in 0.9 seconds!

After looking at chairs for weeks, I had a few real-life experiences that pointed me in the direction of canvas deck chairs. So now my searches were refined by the words "canvas," "French," "folding," "deck chairs" and the like (down to only 79,000 results for "canvas folding deck chair"!).

Digital photography has changed how we view and share images in many ways. Online photo storage is available for free or by subscription and many users allow their photos to be viewed by the public. These online photo-sharing sites are communities of their own—users comment on each other's images, create groups that share images with common themes, and generally support each other's creative development.

When users upload their images, they allocate tags to the images. The tag can be descriptive or classifying or simply name the image. For example, Vincent van Gogh's painting *Van Gogh's Chair* could be tagged "yellow," "blue," "chair," "oil painting," "vincent van gogh," "post impressionism," or "van gogh's chair." Within an online hosting site, I often narrow my searches by selecting particular tags. If I'm in a yellow mood, I may search just the tag "yellow." Among the photos of butter, daffodils, and canaries, there will be Vincent's chair.

It is important to remember that while many photographers choose to allow use of their images in varying forms via Creative Commons licenses, others do not and they retain full copyright ownership of the images. The purpose of viewing images is to stimulate and inspire, not to find something to copy.

Of course, inspiration comes not just in the form of what we see. It's also very much a result of what we think. Helen's quilts are rich in thought and storytelling, excellent examples of the benefits of researching a subject and considering it (with a sharp intellect). Kristin's Chocolate quilt illustrates the fascinating story of the Marquise de Coëtlogon, who in 1671 delivered a biracial baby whose complexion was explained by her excessive consumption of chocolate! While Kristin's research was not Internet-based, it easily could have been. There's a whole crazy World Wide Web out there!

—Kirsten Duncan

Theme 4: Water chosen by: **Karen Rips**

My theme was Water, and I remember at the time wanting to pick a theme that was very broad based, open to lots of different interpretations. I didn't know the other Twelves very well at the time, and I was nervous about picking the "perfect" theme that everyone would be happy with.

Firmament

Rainbows and Sun Breaks

Swimming Pool Reflections

New World

The Creek

Music from Across the Water

Droplets

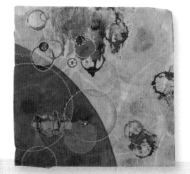

Water: Sustainer and Destroyer

On Top of the World

Coriolis

Splish Splash

Ocean Dreaming

Droplets

Françoise Jamart

For each quilt, I got many ideas that I didn't have time or space to work over. This leaves plenty of possibilities for other pieces. For each theme, I could easily make a journal from all the pages I have written and the sketches I did.

Françoise JANART

Exploring the Theme

I was rather pleased when Karen announced her chosen theme on our blog. Water seemed to offer many possibilities, and lots of ideas came straight away to my mind. First of all, water means life for us human beings. Then I thought of all the different physical states of water, about the rain (we have plenty in Belgium—too much most of the time!), about the pollution and the conservation of water....

When I'm given a theme, I often have a sort of brainstorm and I look for word connections. Although I had already found quite a few potential paths to follow, I decided to do this kind of exploration here as well and to write down everything that came to my mind. I ended up with a page or two filled with words like sea, ocean (hence sailing, silence,

peace, meditation, Buddhism, Zen), blue, green, emerald (like the Côte d'Émeraude in France, which is a favorite vacation place), gray (like the sea in Belgium), stream, flow, energy, life (cycle), waves (Japanese design, sashiko), vortex, spiral, drops, droplets, steam, ice, seawater, fresh water, running water, watercolors.... I also thought of the kanji sign for water.

After a while, I remembered this lovely picture of dew droplets I had taken in my garden. I had already played with it a little before this challenge was issued and I saw it had great potential. Plus, I really liked it. The droplets on the grass blades are very delicate, impermanent. There is a quality about these droplets that makes me think of Buddhism. They are so

Firmament

I used Genesis 1:6 as additional inspiration for the water theme: "And God said, Let there be a firmament in the midst of the waters, and let it divide the waters from the waters." Using this idea of firmament, I created a sweeping arch at the top and used several colors and textures that might invoke water's many powers. Further exploring the idea, I created a fabric accordion book that can be unfolded from the center section of the quilt. On each page, I stamped words for things you can do with water, including bathe, soak, splash, drink, and float.

Deborah Boschert

beautiful and pure, but they are also ephemeral and they can be destroyed very easily at any time. To this day, this picture remains one of my favorites. I know I could use other elements of it in more pieces of work as well. I think the way the water is sitting on top of the mushrooms is quite interesting too, and I love the pattern one can distinguish on the mushrooms caps.

Anyway, for my Water quilt, I decided to concentrate on the leaf and the droplets. I cropped and manipulated the digital image, playing with contrast, luminosity, colors, and a few other effects.

Rainbows and Sun Breaks

Life in Portland, Oregon, means that for much of the year rain is a predominant factor. For me, it was an easy jump from the water theme to weather. In Portland, we have gentle, misty rain with occasional sun breaks and rainbows. So this became my theme. I printed a photo of a rainbow in a landscape on cotton. I then printed a faded version of the same photo on organza. I cut the organza into strips of varying widths. These were fused to the background photo. I overlapped the strips to give a more watery, misty look to represent the rain. I left parts of the background without the organza overlay to represent the sun breaks. The quilting was done to replicate rain and sunshine. I added rainbow fabric to the black border.

Creating the Quilt

First, I printed the picture in large size on white cotton fabric, and also on organza. I chose to do this in blue as it is my favorite color and I'm rather comfortable working with a blue color scheme. I then pieced a first quilt top using the blue image printed on cotton fabric, some fabric I had dyed using onion skins, a dark blue hand-dyed fabric, and also a very traditional Japanese fabric. But I didn't even quilt this top because I didn't find it very interesting. I didn't like the organza print any better; I found it too dull. I wanted the little spark of light in the droplets to show on my quilt. It did very well on paper, but not as well on fabric.

At one point, I thought that maybe I should give up working so closely

from the source picture, and I tried to turn the dead leaf and the grass blades into an abstract design, among other things into a sort of

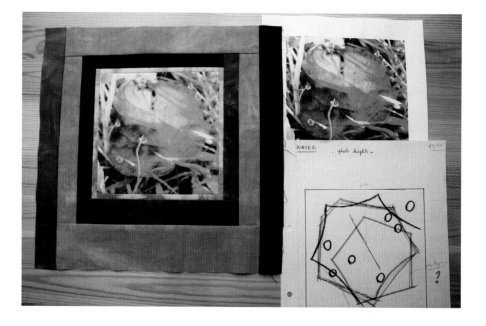

pentagon, without much success.

Then I had the idea to print the picture on banana paper, giving up the blue monochrome scheme and

Swimming Pool Reflections

Midway through this cycle of 12 quilts it dawned on me that what I liked to do was use my art to comment on or raise awareness of social issues. However, at the time of Water I was still a nascent art quilter finding my feet and I struggled to be inspired by the water. In hindsight I could have done better than this image of what I saw as I swam in the pool at my gym. Even the title is boring. However, when the quilt was posted, I was intrigued at the various interpretations of the long blue rectangle by the other Twelves. Whatever the maker intends, the great thing about art is that the viewer interacts with it, bringing her own thoughts and interpretations. Which is a good thing, as the suggestions were far more interesting than the prosaic reality that the rectangle was the door to the toilets!

Helen L Conway

opting for a more natural bicolor image (although the grass is still a bit on the blue side…). This time, I liked the result much better. The colors were great and the texture of the paper added something to the picture. And, after all, why couldn't I use paper in my quilt? I chose to work with three copies of the image. I first picked the background fabric, a hand-dyed cotton, somewhere between yellow and ochre. I bonded the paper images on hand-dyed blue-green fabric squares just a bit larger than the prints, and I kept moving them on the background fabric until I found the most pleasing arrangement to my eyes. In order to make my choice between several options, I often take a lot of pictures and compare them. Sometimes, I also use these work-in-progress pictures to do digital collages for designing. I did this for my Identity quilt (*Weaving New Threads*, page 142); see some examples above.

Back to my Water quilt, I added a few narrow strips of blue-green fabric to complete and balance the design. At that stage, I thought the quilt top didn't need anything more, and I machine-stitched everything down and layered the quilt sandwich. I quilted around the appliquéd images and added a few vertical quilting lines, echoing the blue-green stripes. I then sewed a narrow binding in the same color as the strips and the squares framing my images. As

New World

A few years ago I began to take photos of water. The images contain nothing else but water; what I am recording is the color, the range of which is quite extraordinary. I had no plan for these photos but they became my fabric resource for this quilt. I printed my photos on cloth and then used those fabrics to create an appliqué of the image of my daughter, Ali, taking her first scuba dive on the Barrier Reef. One of the water photos (the bright turquoise-blue) was taken on that dive trip.

Kirsten Duncan

an embellishment, I stitched down a few tiny silvery beads, because I thought they were reminiscent of the shiny droplets. When I work on a small quilt, I usually add the embellishments after the binding because, at such a scale, everything is part of the overall design, even a narrow binding.

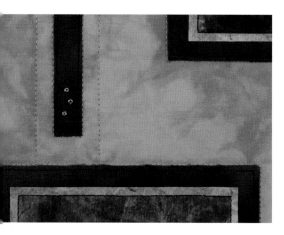

If I had to redo this work today, I would probably decide to add some hand quilting. It is very unusual for me not to use hand stitching in my quilts. Actually, in most of my pieces, I mix hand and machine quilting, and I often use hand embroidery as well because I find it soothing. (See an example at right.) I sometimes think I enjoy the process of designing and sewing the quilt more than the finished work.

I am a bit concerned about the fragility of my Water quilt. Because I used paper, it should not be folded—at least not without being careful—and I'm not really sure how permanent the printing is. Of course, when I made this quilt I had no idea it would be exhibited and would have to travel. On the other hand, I must

The Creek

Our house has a creek running through the property. As we worked on renovating the house through the winter and spring, I watched the water rise and fall and listened to the peaceful sound it made as it burbled along. It is hypnotizing to stand on the little bridge and look down and watch how it swirls past the rocks and carries leaves and bits along. The curves it moves in are graceful and graphic and those are what I decided to focus on. I painted the fabrics for this piece and especially love the rocks.

Terry Grant

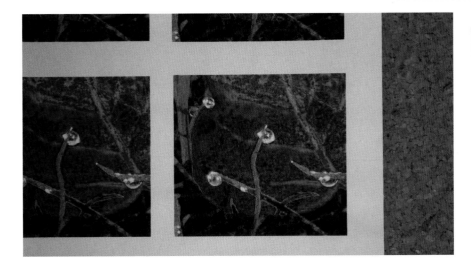

admit that it is certainly not as fragile as Kristin's Water quilt, which was made with the declared purpose of being one day destroyed by splashing water on it. That's why I gave her the award of the Biggest Stretch of the Theme when we did our own awards ceremony on our blog.

Most of the time, I don't print my pictures to use them directly in a quilt. Rather they serve as inspiration for drawing, printing (screenprinting, block printing or stenciling), and embroidering. But here, the image was already so graphic with its very sharp components—the grass blades, the droplets, the shape of the leaf, its veins and stem—that it was very tempting to use it straight away.

My Inspiration

I have always liked to take photographs, but digital photography has really changed my way of seeing the natural world. When I load an image on the computer and I start zooming in, I see many details that I have not seen in real life. It's like discovering a new world. These days, I often find myself looking for subjects to photograph in my garden, especially small things, flowers, leaves, buds, insects, tiny ladybugs (I have a thing for labybugs), or close-ups of tree bark, moss, lichen, etc.

Looking back, I realize that I have used my own photos as sources of inspiration for seven of my Twelve by Twelve quilts: Dandelion, Water, Illumination, Shelter, Window, Identity, and Passion.

Music from Across the Water

When Karen announced this theme, I knew that I wanted to illustrate the theme with minimal use of the color blue. Perhaps it was the contrary side of my personality revealing itself, but I also wanted to avoid lapsing into the literal depiction I struggle to avoid. After searching through photographs, I found beautiful and colorful photographs of reflections on water by Russell Docksteader. With Russell's permission, I translated his image into fabric using fabric paints and machine stitching. You can see more of Russell Docksteader's photography at www.flickr.com/photos/rldock

Diane Perin Hock

In addition to Mother Nature, my main sources of inspiration are my close family and the relationships we have, and my travels. I'm in love with Japan and its traditions, its ancient and modern crafts, and its textile handiwork. I'm fascinated by its language, especially its writing system, and I'm intrigued by its religious practices.

I don't think I really work in series, but one piece almost always inspires or at least influences the next one. Also, I mainly use my own hand-dyed fabrics and I try to keep my designs as simple as possible. These are probably the reasons why my fellow Twelves kept saying that I was building a coherent body of work with my Twelve by Twelve pieces, although it took me some time to become aware of this.

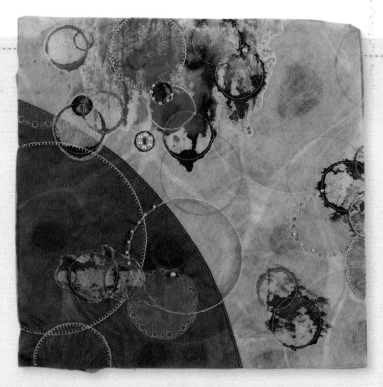

Water: Sustainer & Destroyer

Life cannot exist without water, yet water has the power to destroy as well. To convey that, I created this piece out of elements affected by water. The base is water-soluble stabilizer colored with water-based paints. The backing is marbled fabric created by floating paint on water. It is stitched with water-soluble thread and the pearls were adhered with temporary glue. Additional details were added with watercolor pencils and a marker that disappears when wet. Currently the piece represents the sustaining quality of water. Eventually, I'll show water's destructive side by dousing the art.

Kristin LaFlamme

Working with the Twelves

Being part of this small group of art quilters proved to be a very good incentive to work on a regular basis. I do not enter many shows or competitions, and it's not always easy to keep being motivated when you don't show your work and you don't have many interested people around to share it with. So, when Diane asked me if I wanted to be part of the group, I think I was ready for it, and I said yes of course. I like to work small, and the challenge was to make a small art quilt every other month on a given theme. This was just the amount of stimulation I needed. I already knew some of the other members through their blogs. I had exchanged emails with Brenda, I had been part of an online group with Terri and Diane was the initiator of the Artful Quilters Blog Ring that I was a member of. I had even met Kristin in real life back when she was still living in Germany: I went to Heidelberg to see the Third European Quilt Triennial. Kristin had a show at a small gallery at the same time, so this was the perfect opportunity to meet her. I "knew" her because I was reading her blog, and we had already exchanged a few emails on this and that.

Since the Twelve by Twelve group has been set up, I have briefly met Helen twice in Birmingham, at the Festival of Quilts. And when Karen and her husband visited Paris, I jumped at the opportunity to travel to France to meet her. It was funny that we met in a French-speaking city, and that, for once, I felt very at home and at ease. Indeed, in the Twelve by Twelve group, I am the only one whose native language is not English, and from time to time, it's a bit hard for me. I sometimes find it difficult to express myself as precisely and subtly in English as I can in French, especially in a direct conversation or a quick email exchange, and I'm sure that sometimes I accidentally say things that I don't mean. But luckily my fellow Twelves seem to bear with me!

Frankly, the way our group remained motivated and kept up with the deadlines surprised me a little. I had already been part of a few online groups, and often they don't stand the test of time. Here, we all kept the pace and didn't miss one single deadline. Over time, a kind of friendship (or should I say fellowship?) has developed between us. And I am delighted that we have decided to continue the adventure and that we are now working on a new series of Twelve by Twelve quilts.

On Top of the World

After having picked the theme, I had the hardest time coming up with an idea. I looked through my photos from our travels and settled on this picture I took while at Lake Titicaca, which straddles Peru and Bolivia. I quilted white silk/cotton fabric then painted in the features. Hand stitching was used to indicate the reeds that grow on the shores of the lake.

Karen L. Rips

I certainly didn't expect all this to happen when I started my blog, after much hesitation, in 2006. I had been reading a few blogs for some months, and I was eager to show my work to like-minded people. I thought it would also be a good way to keep track of my work. I didn't think I would meet that many people in cyberspace, much less in real life.

Working for this challenge gave me lots of potential ideas. For each quilt, I got many ideas that I didn't have time or space to work over. This leaves plenty of possibilities for other pieces. For each theme, I could easily make a journal from all the pages I have written and the sketches I did. Actually, I already started doing this for some of them. I enjoy working in sketchbooks, painting, printing,

Coriolis

At first, I experimented with shibori to create "water" fabric. As I rinsed the fabrics, I observed turquoise water disappearing down the drain. This reinforced my decision to concentrate on this quilt. Coriolis is my tribute to the enduring myth that water goes down the drain in a different direction depending which hemisphere you are in. (Apparently, the Coriolis force is real but is noticeable only for large-scale motions such as winds.) My techniques included freehand cutting and piecing, hand-stitched embellishment in perle cotton and variegated threads, and a mitred-facing finish. *Brenda Gael Smith*

and collaging, even if I usually don't show them to anybody. Now, an idea that could fit in a 12 x12-inch (30.5 x 30.5 cm) quilt will not necessarily work on a larger one. But thanks to this group, I've got a whole list of paths to explore. This should help me in trying to reach my artistic goals for the coming years: to keep learning new surface design techniques, experiment with different color schemes (that should be easy with the next Twelve by Twelve Colorplay series!), work more with texture and hand embroidery, and maybe build a cohesive body of work.

I would like to thank Diane for her initiative, Brenda for helping the group keep the momentum, and all the members for the support and stimulation.

Splish Splash

I am a fan of artist Nellie Durand. I love her use of fabrics and the landscapes she creates. Nellie's work was the inspiration for my water quilt. I used blue fabric strips to create the water. I threw in bits of fibers here and there to give the look of waves and foam as you see at the beach. I had always wanted to create a mermaid figure and this was my chance. I drew her on paper and then created templates for each of her body parts. I added fibers to give her hair more texture, beads and sequins to add pizzazz to her lower body, and drew in her facial features with fabric markers. Lastly, I added teardrop pearl beads to give the illusion of water drops spraying off her tail.

Terri Stegmiller

TAKE IT FURTHER

Several Twelves have used at least one or more of their Twelve by Twelve quilts as a springboard to other work. The techniques Brenda used in her Mathematics piece (*Binary Note #2*, page 102) led to a series named Dreamlines.

One of her candidate quilts for the same challenge she found too abstract for the theme (but nevertheless liked) inspired her series Desire Lines. Her quilt *Desire Lines #2: Caliente* (page 157), made for the Passion theme, is part of this series. For the Water theme, she experimented with shibori dyeing and she subsequently used some of the resulting fabrics in two quilts. And she's also been working on a larger quilt based on *Radiance* (page 66).

After making her Identity quilt (*Latent Color*, page 141), Diane wanted to make a larger finger-print quilt. She completed it a few months later as an assignment for a workshop she was taking.

The quilt Deborah made for the Illumination challenge (*The Fourth Day*, page 67) was already a sort of continuation of her interpretation of the Water theme (*Firmament*, page 54). She liked it so much that she decided to start a series of art quilts incorporating elements from illuminated manuscripts.

Kristin used the composition of her Dande-lion piece (*Löwenzahn und Pusteblume*, page 18) as the starting point for the composition of a larger quilt that she completed two years later. And after painting her Window quilt (*Defenestration*, page 121) she felt confident enough to paint her Twelve quilt (*12 Months*, page 168) too.

My pink quilt, made for the first challenge of our second series, *Colorplay*, was the inspiration for a larger work. I had a lot of screen-printed fabrics left over from the project, so I decided to make another quilt in the same spirit but in a larger format. I finally had to dye more fabric in the same color scheme, but in solid colors, because I found out that the screen-printed fabric—which was perfect for a small quilt—was too busy to be used on a larger scale. The new quilt is about 32 x 32 inches (81 x 81 cm). And I still have some more screen-printed fabric that I plan to use in fiber postcards and bookmarks, and maybe in small quilts.

—Françoise Jamart

Magic Carpet
by Brenda Gael Smith

Making a Good Impression
by Diane Perin Hock

Rosebud Quilt
(in progress)
by Françoise Jamart

Ocean Dreaming

I love the ocean. It is so alive with winter storms and glistening sunshine. The perfect place for quiet reflection and adventurous exploration. Its vastness quickly brings perspective to life's troubles. I dream of leisurely days walking on the beach and gazing out to sea, with its waves crashing. I know my romantic vision leaves out the devastating potential of the ocean, but isn't that what dreams are for?

I created my quilt with hand-painted fabrics that I quilted with blue metallic thread. I then cut them to fit and zigzag stitched the edges together.

Nikki Wheeler

Theme 5: **Illumination**

chosen by: **Brenda Gael Smith**

I eschewed physical objects in favor of words that invited abstract exploration and different interpretations. My shortlist included "cosmos," "stories," and "enigma." Then I was reading about Paris (the City of Light) and, in a flash of inspiration, I had a new word and my chosen theme—Illumination.

The Fourth Day

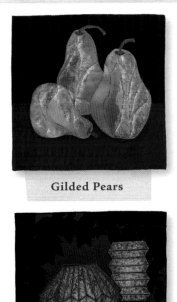

Gilded Pears

Blackpool Rocks

Dappled

Japanese Lanterns

Happy Lanterns

Meditation

Night Light

Enlightenment

Radiance

Click

Illumination Celebration

Feature Quilt

Radiance

Brenda Gael Smith

Embracing the serendipity factor, I willingly surrender to the surprise of shibori. Indeed, this applies to my quiltmaking generally—I seldom plan an entire project before I begin and I love to work spontaneously, making design decisions and little discoveries along the way.

In the Beginning

With the impulse to create comes the desire to share, so it's not surprising that my online activity and website presence has developed in step with my quiltmaking and is manifest in the Twelve by Twelve Collaborative Art Quilt Project.

When I first started patchwork and quilting, my youngest brother helped me set up a basic website displaying images of my quilts for viewing by friends and family in New Zealand and elsewhere. Soon I moved the site to my own domain. The website expanded rapidly as, enthused with a digital camera I had received as a farewell gift from work colleagues, I added scores of photos of my coursework from the online City & Guilds patchwork and quilting course I was undertaking at the time.

Looking back, I was really just a frustrated blogger attempting real-time glimpses into my creative progress using a clumsy combination of my website and e-mail notifications to anyone that might be interested. Blogging was an emerging phenomenon. Inspired by Diane's blog and others on the Artful Quilters Blog Ring, I celebrated my final retirement from legal practice by setting up my own blog in late 2005. I soon established a warm online dialogue with Diane, Kirsten, Françoise, and Helen, and became a regular reader of the blogs of Gerrie, Kristin, and Deborah.

Fortunately, Helen alerted me to Diane's e-mail that had been diverted to the junk folder of a seldom-used e-mail account. Headed, "NEW

Brenda Gael Smith

The Fourth Day

I created a modern illuminated art quilt for this theme. It's inspired by ancient illuminated manuscripts with their foil accents, scroll-like designs, and blocks of text. I referenced the fourth day of creation from Genesis 1:16, "God made two great lights—the greater light to govern the day and the lesser light to govern the night." I used elements of darkness and light, stars and circles in this fiber collage. I especially love the gold monoprint on the black background. It's like an expanse of darkness swirling into being.

Deborah Boschert

small quilt challenge: Wanna play?", Diane's invitation was at once tantalizing and slightly daunting. I was completing a hectic three-year term on the committee of my local Guild and was looking forward to spending some more "me" time in my studio. Participating in this project seemed like an interesting way of giving some focus to my quiltmaking with sufficient flexibility to explore different techniques and styles that appeal to me. Yet I was also wary of the commitment involved, especially since I'd never worked at this small scale and always struggle to make quilts to a particular size.

After some reflection, I decided that the risk of the challenge fizzling out in the ashes of good intentions was outweighed by its promise—that is, we can each work on our quilts in our own time, but with the discipline and momentum of a fixed deadline, and still bounce off the creative energy that is generated by working with an enthusiastic group. I had little inkling of just how rewarding the experience would be.

Selecting the Theme

From the outset of the Twelve by Twelve project, I collected potential themes in anticipation of my turn to set the challenge. The four prior themes were botanical, gastronomical, sociological, and elemental, but that left me plenty of scope. I had many ideas but I was still feeling a little anxious about choosing the "right" one that was not too predictable. I sought a theme that was neither so prescriptive as to thwart imagination nor so broad or obscure as to be overwhelming for our two-month challenge

Gilded Pears

While leafing through an art magazine, I was struck by still lifes that just seemed to glow. This technique is known as chiaroscuro. I had some wonderful hand-dyed silk that just screamed pears. They looked illuminated even before the foiling, but I decided to add the foil for this challenge! The background is dupioni silk.

Gennie Congdon

timeframe. I eschewed physical objects in favor of words that invited abstract exploration and different interpretations. My shortlist included "cosmos," "stories," and "enigma." Then I was reading about Paris (the City of Light) and, in a flash of inspiration, I had a new word and my chosen theme—Illumination.

I no longer practice law but I retain my love of words and rich, expansive definitions. Consulting a dictionary, I found that illumination is a multi-faceted noun. It refers to the act of illuminating, the state of being illuminated, decorative lighting, or a source of light. It also covers notions of spiritual or intellectual enlightenment and the process of clarification or elucidation. Finally it even has an artistic angle—the act of decorating a text, page, or initial letter with ornamental designs, miniatures, or lettering.

Making a Start

Despite selecting the theme, illumination remained elusive. Various commitments kept me away from the studio for much of the Illumination challenge period and I made fewer pieces than I did for other challenges. Part of me would like to say that I spent this time out and about, sketching, composing, and recording ideas in my visual diary to tap into upon my return—but the truth is that I rarely work in this fashion. Mostly I prefer to carry ideas in my head, or on my computer; work directly with my materials; and let a piece evolve

Blackpool Rocks

I learned to quilt in relative isolation, which means that I was not influenced by the Quilt Police's conception of what a quilt should look like. I soon took the view that if it would stick on somehow, it could go on. In the Northwest of England, "the illuminations" refers to an extravaganza of lights and tableaux strung along the Blackpool beach in an attempt to extend the tourist season. It is brash and glittery, fun and bright. By day, when the bulbs are dimmed, Blackpool is a town with serious problems, its economy appearing to limp along on selling tattoos and the local confectionary "rock" that comes on sticks with words embedded in it. The light wand represents the illuminations and also Blackpool Tower (a poor imitation of the Eiffel Tower). Underneath are cross sections of rock, the usual "love me true" and "kiss me quick" mottos replaced with grim statistics about Blackpool's reality.

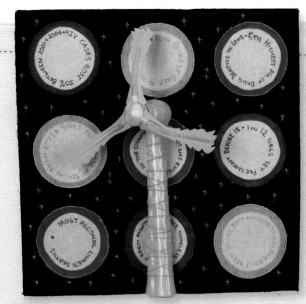

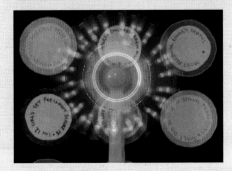

on the design wall. Mindful that a working journal might be interesting for future Twelve by Twelve exhibition purposes, I did actually jot down some inspiration in a shiny new book but that's as far as it went. I have a whole section in my bookshelf dedicated to barely-touched journals!

Fledgling ideas included moonlight, sunrise, theatre lights, streetlights, lanterns, candles, and neon lights. Even small quilts can be surprisingly time-consuming to conceive and execute, and false starts are not unusual. Following the death of my grandmother, and going through her belongings with my family, I found a simple black and gold cut-out stencil silhouette of a woman looking down—a kind of optical illusion that I remember squinting at many times as a child. I transferred the image to

Dappled

The small pools of color here are silk pieces that I dyed with pigment inks then burned (over a candle) to make irregular shapes. I first imagined this quilt to be dense and covered in these little circles, as it is representative of the thick daubs of oil paint used by the Impressionists to represent light. I positioned the silk, building up the fabric as with paint. It looked awful. I removed most of them until it approximated the look I wanted. If I had allowed myself more time, I would have remade this quilt with a more interesting background.

Kirsten Duncan

fabric using paint sticks and a freezer paper stencil. I considered using this as the basis of the Illumination quilt but soon realized that most people perceived mere blobs rather than the illuminated outline of the woman's features. I quilted around the "blobs" of the copper version and experimented with some grid quilting in the background but the remaining puffiness bugged me, as did the propensity of black fabric to catch lint and dust.

Besides, once again, I was attracted to exploring a theme in shibori. This involves some domestic negotiation and a clearance to use the wet area in my husband's workshop, as I generally make more mess than he is entirely comfortable with and I gave up dyeing in the main house long ago.

When my husband and I decided to move to our beach house full time and leave the city behind, we built an extension to include a dedicated quilting studio for me and a work-shop for him. My studio has an enormous window along one wall providing abundant natural light and a panoramic view over Copacabana Beach. That light is integral to life and

color—especially a vibrant, creative life—is a daily revelation as I observe the ever-changing patterns on the surface of the water created by light, waves, currents (and whales!), and remark upon how light conditions change the mood of the day.

Whereas my Dandelion quilt (*Pièce de Résistance*, page 20) was created using stitching resists, for Illumina-

Japanese Lanterns

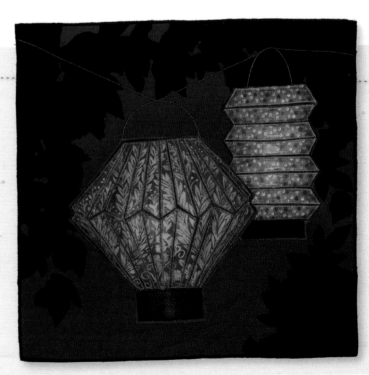

Light is most striking when it shines out of darkness. It draws us to it and speaks to us at a very basic level. I think of turn-ing onto my street late at night and seeing my porch light glowing in the darkness. All is well. We are home. I long to sit out among the trees in the darkness, under the stars, and I can imagine glowing paper lanterns lighting our way through the shadows.

Terry Grant

Happy Lanterns

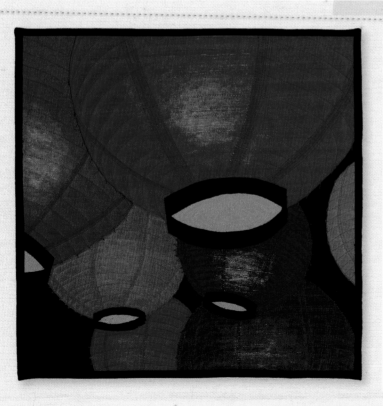

Perhaps because of my happy memories of our trip to China to adopt our daughter in 1996, I am drawn to images from Chinese culture. I have always loved the look of paper lanterns too—they convey such an immediate sense of festivity. Illustrating boldly colored lanterns was a natural choice for the Illumination theme. After drawing out my composition, I cut and fused pieces of dupioni silk for the lantern globes. The ribs and the spines of each lantern were defined with machine stitching and fabric crayons. Judicious coloring with a yellow pastel crayon "lit" the lanterns and keeps them glowing. I was surprised and delighted to see that Terry Grant also illustrated lanterns for her Illumination piece, with a different look from mine.

Diane Perin Hock

tion I decided to use simple fold resists to create lantern designs, applying black dye to gold fabrics. I experimented with different kinds of folds and pleats. For some pieces I soaked the fabric in soda ash and let the fabric dry thoroughly before applying the dye; for others I applied the dye while the fabric was wet. Embracing the serendipity factor, I willingly surrender to the surprise and serendipity of shibori. Indeed, this applies to my quiltmaking generally—I seldom plan an entire project before I begin, and love to work spontaneously, making design decisions and little discoveries along the way. I ended up with some dramatic results and auditioned them on my design wall.

My 6 x 6-foot (1.8 x 1.8-m) design wall is integral to my quiltmaking, and my digital camera and computer also make indispensible companions. I selected this piece from my shibori samples because the central motif serendipitously fit in a 12 x 12 (30.5 x 30.5 cm) square, and because of its Zen feel—another play on the theme word.

A lantern in the darkness radiates the promise of life and sanctuary,

Meditation

For this quilt, I chose to work on the Buddhist meaning of illumination. My background fabric was shibori-dyed. I drew a very simple shape of someone sitting and meditating, and with that shape I made a stencil out of freezer paper. I used oil sticks to print the shapes and their shadows on my fabric. I added a little yellow paint in some of the white spots of the dyed fabric and embroidered small stars.

Françoise JANART

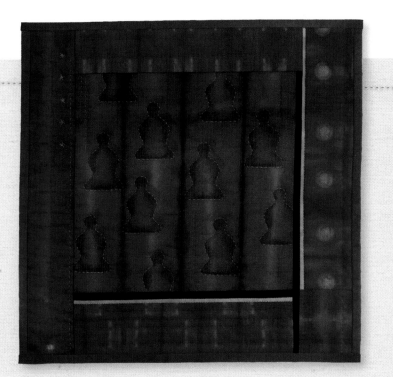

and I enhanced the effect of glimmering light with hand stitching in variegated thread.

Since then, I have had plenty of practice making those small stitch-es, as I have completed a 6-inch (15.2-cm) "mini" Radiance piece for each of the Twelves and also made a larger work, *Shining Through*, from one of the lantern shibori fabrics.

Ironically (given the theme), on the eve of the reveal of the Illumination works our blog was effectively plunged into darkness for 72 hours, as a technical glitch with our

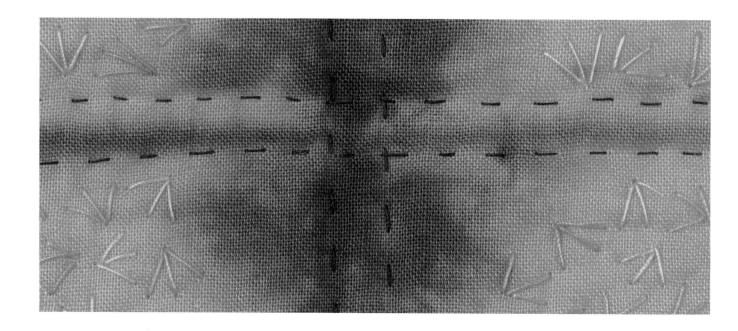

Night Light

What do you remember doing as a child after the lights went out? And what does it have to do with quilting? In the illumination of a flashlight under the covers, I think it's safe to say that we've all found some sort of enlightenment in favorite novels, pulp fiction, or comics. This two-sided quilt features a traditional Sunshine and Shadows tied quilt on one side and a portrait of a reading child on the other, stitched free-motion with my sewing machine.

Kristin LaFlamme

blogging platform locked us out and prevented us from publishing new posts. This enforced blackout added to the suspense, but there was light at the end of the tunnel.

I prepare the images for the group's dedicated website gallery, and each time I compile the thumbnails I am astounded at how our independently created works combine to make such a cohesive, collaborative quilt mosaic. In the case of the Illumination theme, the mosaic is unified by a palette of gold, blue, and black, with red highlights. Even the bright lights of Helen's piece are complemented by the multi-colored fragments in Kirsten's quilt. And the way Terri's light bulb echoes the shape of Gerrie's pears is magical.

In setting the theme, I had hoped that the multiple meanings of "illumination" would encourage diverse responses. I was not disappointed! The talent and imagination of the Twelves came shining through.

Enlightenment

Enlightenment is another form of Illumination. Internal rather than external, enlightenment encompasses the ideas of clarity, reflection, and serenity. This image of the Buddha includes all of that to me. I happen to have a large collection of East Indian fabrics, including saris that I have been purchasing over the years, and this seemed like the perfect opportunity to use some of them.

Karen L. Rips

Helen and Kristin presented dynamic, interactive quilts. Despite being in the midst of the upheaval of moving from Germany to Hawaii, Kristin created an imaginative double-sided work with a traditional Sunshine and Shadows design on one side and a thread drawing of her son under covers, reading by flashlight, on the other. Once again, Helen demonstrated her inventive use of materials and layers of meaning—the playful colors of the whirling light wand belying the illuminatingly grim social statistics of the seaside resort of Blackpool. Françoise and Karen picked up on the element of spiritual enlightenment. With a clarity and serenity that typifies much of Françoise's work, she incorporated a simple shape of someone sitting and meditating. Karen used an image of Buddha and shimmery East Indian fabrics, although an unfortunate encounter between a hot iron and the delicate sari material left her feeling less than Zen for a while.

Terry could hardly believe her eyes when she saw Diane's gaily colored round lanterns, a happy complement to the angled paper lanterns in Terry's design. Meanwhile, Terri presented a lifelike electric light bulb complete with ball chain that you can almost hear going "click."

Both Gerrie and Kirsten drew upon artistic depictions of light. Kirsten captured dappled light in the style of the Impressionists while Gerrie referenced the bold contrasts of the chiaroscuro technique to create voluptuous, glowing pears.

Deborah created an illuminated page illustrating the verse from Genesis where God created lights in the sky to separate the day from the night, and to serve as signs to mark seasons and days and years. The sun, the greater light, governs the day and the lesser light and stars govern the night.

Images from day and night inspired Nikki's Illumination Celebration that is based on photos of the sunlight shining through the trees in her garden and the flash of fireworks in the darkness.

Shine! From St. Paul to the Beach Boys and St. Thomas Aquinas to the Rolling Stones, the invocation to let your light show has been a powerful message throughout the ages. In the 21st century, we are fortunate that the Internet and other technologies enable us to share our creative endeavors and to reach out around the world.

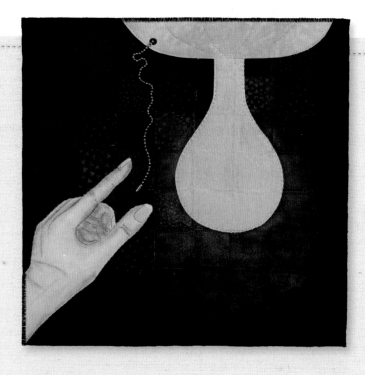

Click

Nothing says Illumination more to me than the sudden turning on of a light. When I was young, I remember my grandparents' home had lights just like these in some of the basement rooms. I started with squares of dark-colored fabrics on the background. I used a silk fabric for the light bulb and I hand-dyed a fabric for the hand. The details on the hand were drawn on with pen, and shading and highlights were added with paint. I dry-brushed yellow paint on and around the light bulb for the illuminated effect. I couched on the ball chain to give the illusion of it springing back after clicking the light on. *Terri Stegmiller*

TWELVE REASONS TO BLOG

Sharing your creative life online is now easier than ever. Popular free, hosted blogging platforms such as Blogger (www.blogger.com) and WordPress (www.wordpress.com) offer the ability to set up a simple website that includes both a dynamic blog component and separate static pages for content such as your resume or quilt gallery. And the good news is that you can administer your site yourself without the need for extensive technical expertise.

Quilters have been quick to embrace the potential of blogging. Here are twelve reasons why you might like to give it a go:

1. Personal expression. Bold or reserved, vibrant or subdued, playful or serious, thoughtful or flippant? There is room in the blogosphere for everyone. Your blog is another form of self-expression and you get to set your own parameters. How liberating!

2. Community. Whether you live in the city or the remote outback or somewhere in between, you can engage with others from all over the world and true friendships can flourish. If you prefer something more intimate, you can restrict access to your blog to people that you know, or you can keep your blog completely private.

3. Encouragement. When others around you are bored with or oblivious to your creative endeavors, there is always someone in blogland to cheer you on and celebrate your achievement.

4. Accountability. A public statement of intention can also help keep you motivated.

5. Problem solving. If you are stuck, blog about it and all sorts of creative solutions may emerge.

6. Critique. Readers will often provide constructive feedback—especially if you ask for it.

7. Trend spotting. Keep up to date with the latest techniques and products.

8. Education. Reading and writing tutorials, and analysis, are instructive processes.

9. Record keeping. Track the development of a particular project; store inspirational images; recall the date of a particular event—it's all there in your blog archives.

10. Profile raising. Share your work online, reach a wider audience, and enhance your profile.

11. Opportunity. Make it easy for people to find out more about you and your art, and this may lead to unexpected opportunities such as exhibitions, sales, or even a publishing contract.

12. And it's fun—what are you waiting for?!

—Brenda Gael Smith

Illumination Celebration

My inspiration was from photos of fireworks I took on the Fourth of July and a wonderful photo of the sun rising through the trees in my backyard. Fireworks seemed appropriate given that they were referred to as "illuminations" at the time of the original Fourth of July.

To create my quilt, I painted the background; for the light burst, I used metallic paints and added thread painting with metallic thread. I finished the edges with a fuzzy yarn.

Nikki Wheeler

Theme 6: Shelter

chosen by: **Terri Stegmiller**

How basic is the idea of shelter? Shelter is one of those things we don't think about much until it is needed. I chose this theme knowing there were so many ways it could be portrayed and I couldn't wait to see how the other Twelves interpreted it.

Cedar and Stone

Rainy Day Shelter

Shelter

Everlasting

A Roof Over My Head

First Shelter

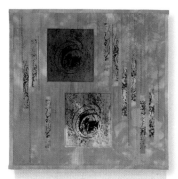
Two Snails on a Tree

Shelter From The Storm

Lost City

Favela

Rooms for Rent

Backpacking...in Rhinestone Heels

Feature Quilt

Lost City

Karen Rips

One does not have to be a world traveler to find the spark that begins the artistic process. I have always been intrigued by the micro world and constantly take close-up photos of everything from flowers to barbed wire. Yet as an artist, I have been greatly influenced by my travels.

I Am a Twelve, I Am an Artist!

I always had a problem thinking of myself as an artist until I became a Twelve. It was a concept that I could not quite wrap my mind around. On the most basic level I am a woman, a wife, and a mother, which I paid tribute to in my work for the Identity theme (*Female*, at the right and on page 144). These are, of course, those traditional labels that we occasionally embrace, yet sometimes feel were inflicted upon us by others. I am also comfortable calling myself a nurse, my chosen profession. Yet, as a person who on a regular basis creates tangible art using screen-printed images, dyed cloth, threads, cheesecloth, and various other textured surfaces, I found it difficult to accept that I was in fact creating art. The Twelves changed all that for me.

The idea of a challenge group is nothing new to blogdom but I do believe this group is special. First and foremost, we have had the discipline to keep at it for two years. Deadlines were met and the "unveilings" became something each of us and many other fiber artists have looked forward to. In fact over the last two years we have developed somewhat of a following. It has been noted that there are a number of individuals that have mirrored our themes, and some newly formed groups have mentioned us as their inspiration. Our own friends and families have watched us develop with great pride. Secondly, the Twelves are a diverse group artistically, geographically, politically, and chronologically. This group has been nurturing

Cedar and Stone

When I lived in Maine, I fell in love with stones. The rock walls found near roadsides, forests, and hiking trails are beautiful in their color, texture, construction, and history. Exploring these ideas, I found a beautiful picture of an Adirondack shelter. It was nestled in green trees, made of simple cedar planks, with a beautiful stone chimney. I abstracted these elements to create this piece. A bit of black tulle is reminiscent of the strong shadows created by the structure.

and complementary rather than competitive.

Its very nature has been to encourage and bring out the best in each other's work. All of these factors have gone into making the Twelves a success. The Twelves have given me the self-confidence to proclaim, "I am a Twelve, I am an artist!"

When we first started this adventure more than two years ago, I had no idea the friendships that would come out of it. Sometimes when the emails are flying back and forth, we seem just like family. I have been fortunate enough to meet five of the Twelves personally, and it has been so much fun to follow the others on their own personal blogs and websites.

Rainy Day Shelter

Recalling a photo looking down on a red umbrella with just a pair of boots visible on the rainy sidewalk, I kept making umbrellas from different silk fabrics, trying to get just the right one. Then I had an epiphany that a trio of umbrellas would make a more interesting composition. I bought raindrop-shaped beads and different paints to try to make the whole thing look rainier. In the end, I decided that the hand-dyed sidewalk fabrics and the umbrellas would be enough to evoke the feeling of rain. The background is hand-dyed cotton. The umbrellas are silk—from hand-dyed fabrics and a vintage Japanese textile. The images are fused and satin stitched.

Examining the Theme

When I look back at the eleven other Shelter pieces, I find a few commonalities in all the pieces, such as the frequent use of simple shapes like squares, rectangles, or triangles, —with the notable exception of my own. The other is more subtle, and relates to the definition of shelter as home, a place of comfort, and safety.

I noticed that the Shelter pieces created by Brenda, Helen, Kristin, and to a certain extent Diane used traditional courthouse-steps or log-cabin designs. The shelter pieces of the remaining seven Twelves were also constructed using simple shapes, either in the foreground or background. My thinking on this is that shelter ultimately reminds us of home, exemplified by square houses, triangular roofs, and rectangular doors. My deviation from this overall trend could be attributed to my particular thought of shelter being more transient than permanent (perhaps I was subliminally influenced by the fact that three of the Twelves were either buying, selling, or moving during the time that shelter was the theme).

When challenged to create art within the confinement of a particular theme, it is my habit to understand the most accepted definition of the word, and then check a thesaurus for alternate meanings. When the theme Shelter was introduced, I initially visualized park benches, shopping carts, cardboard lean-tos, and the homeless shelters you see on big city skid rows. However, my mind quickly found shelter in the more comfortable images of hearth, home, and the individual family. While the standard meaning of the word revolves around the idea of protection, shelter can alternately be used in the context of hiding or providing sanctuary for someone or something. This is when it became

Shelter

This quilt hated me and I hated it. It did not want to be made. I forced it into being, fighting it and my machine all the way. I made a firm base and side flaps out of Pelmet Vilene (an interfacing not available in the U.S), and then quilted it with barbed-wire patterns to create a structure over which a traditionally soft quilt top could be raised to form an actual shelter. Some of the strips are printed with words from the United Nations Declaration on Human Rights; the log cabin blocks are arranged in the courthouse steps pattern, both referring to the concept of law as a shelter from persecution. Inside the shelter I placed what I had believed to be a copyright-free photo relating to the Holocaust. Only, when my Mum saw it she immediately (and, as it transpired, correctly) identified the photo as a very copyrighted image still. So now, no one is allowed to look inside my secret shelter!

Helen L Conway

apparent to me that shelter could have a transitory nuance.

Having alternate "shelter concepts," it then occurred to me to expand my thinking from the individual or familial level to include groups or civilizations of people. This thinking process inevitably led me to my travel photos and then to the lost, hidden city of Machu Picchu.

Machu Picchu is one of those places I had always dreamed of going to, and it lived up to my every expectation. When you approach the site, you literally walk around a corner to the classic view of this abandoned civilization, and it takes your breath away. The structures are laid out in front of you, almost as if the population just got up

Everlasting

The concept of shelter that returned to me again and again as I considered this theme was that of the shelter of love. Lyrics to a favorite hymn say, "Everlasting arms of love are beneath, around, above..." A childhood spent in the shelter of a loving family has an everlasting benefit in one's life. This abstract quilt is an aerial schematic diagram of my childhood home, including the side-by-side houses of my parents and grandparents, the sandpit my Dad made for us, special trees and gardens, and even my grandfather's truck.

Kirsten Duncan

Inspiration for My Quilt

and walked off one day, which is apparently what they did. Built around 1460 by the Incan civilization, it was abandoned only 100 years later when the Spanish invaded Peru. It was rediscovered in 1911 by archeologist Hiram Bingham and is now being preserved by the Peruvian people. Despite their efforts, the site has been crumbling under the number of visitors it receives. Designated a "World Heritage Site," efforts are underway to preserve and restore Machu Picchu by limiting access.

The inspiration for art is all around us. Many artists find their voice in the natural world, others from the spiritual. Some people focus on the human body, the human mind, or the accomplishments and residue left over from human existence. I consider Lost City special because its inspiration, Machu Picchu, embodies all of this. The site is physically, spiritually, and emotionally exhilarating—and is totally engulfed in a natural setting that is difficult to clearly take in.

Most writers refer to Machu Picchu as a lost city. It is now believed that Machu Picchu was more of a religious center or spiritual retreat than

a functioning city or military outpost. It is also speculated that rather than being "lost," it was "hidden," and then abandoned to avoid discovery.

By chance my husband and I found ourselves in Machu Picchu on the summer solstice.

We were there to witness the very first ray of sunlight dance upon the point of an Andean mountain peak, and then illuminate the top of a stone whose shadow created a point which—for just a moment—pointed precisely due west. This event would not happen again until the winter solstice.

One does not have to be a world traveler to find the spark that begins

A Roof Over My Head

The theme of Shelter could relate to only one thing for me—home. My husband and I had spent the past year remodeling and moving into a new-to-us home. It was a difficult year and discouraging in many ways as the housing market deteriorated and the decline of the economy threw us all into a state of anxiety. Still, home is and must be a shelter from the outside world and a refuge from anxiety and fear.

Terry Grant

First Shelter

As often happens for me on these challenges, I had one idea in mind but when I sat down to work on it, another popped into my head that caused me to veer in a totally different direction. As the deadline approached I found myself thinking about caves. I sorted through my stash for black, gray, and brown batiks, thinking that their patterns would work well to convey the natural texture of rock. Once I laid them out to blend from light to dark, I formed the cave walls by folding, placing, and twisting the strips in a very unstructured log-cabin style. Layering and twisting the folds created dimension and solidity to the cave that I really liked. I added the light streaming in with thread stitching. As I created this piece, I was inside the cave looking out. But many viewers have seen it as being outside a cave looking in. Which do you see?

Diane Perin Hock

Coming Up with Ideas

the artistic process. I have always been intrigued by the micro world and constantly take close-up photos of everything from flowers to barbed wire. Yet as an artist, I have been greatly influenced by my travels. I have been artistically energized most everywhere I have been—by the multi-colored buildings in Tangiers, the raft people who live on Lake Titicaca, and in graveyards around the world.

Each time a new theme was introduced, I spent days mulling over the possibilities. My creative process often involves finding one of the thousands of photos that my husband or I have taken, whether it was on an exotic overseas adventure or a simple outing to our favorite Mexican restaurant just an hour away. Sometimes I will be drawn to a particular symbol or even a simple shape, as I did with *Similar Differences* (at the right and on page 47) for our Community theme. Occasionally my work is topical, that is, responsive to events around me. Sometimes it is influenced by places I have visited that are particularly meaningful to

me, such as the Peace Park in Hiroshima, Japan, that inspired *Man's Darkest Side Through the Windows of Hope*, for the Window theme (at the far right and on page 129).

My Twelve by Twelve pieces are pretty much evenly divided between topical, photo-inspired, and symbolic. In my own mind, however, I tend to feel that these distinctions are fairly unimportant. I believe that my art and whatever reaction or emotion it may invoke is the property of whoever is looking at the piece. As an artist, I am very technique oriented, and ultimately it is the cloth, dyes, paints, and threads that dictate the finished product.

Two Snails on a Tree

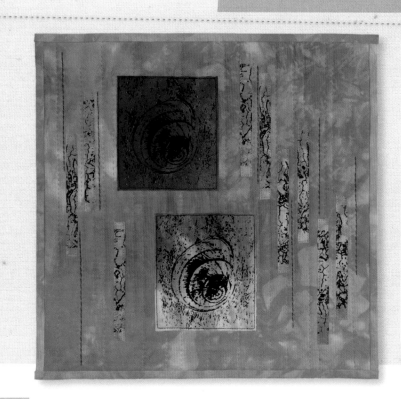

Some time ago, I took many pictures of a tiny snail slowly traveling on a huge tree. I thought these images would make a good starting point for this challenge. The little shell and the big tree offer shelter to the fragile baby snail. I felt the little creature was looking very lonely all by himself. That's why there are two snails on my quilt. The snails were screen-printed on a hand-dyed fabric. I stitched them down by machine and then added hand quilting and embroidery.

Françoise JANART

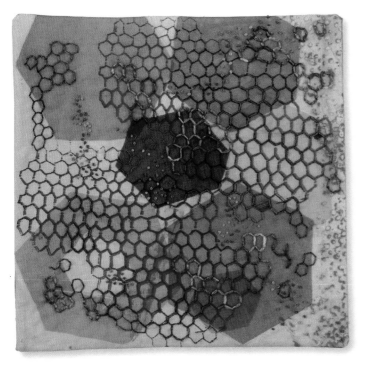

Shelter From The Storm

This quilt was inspired by a view of large tropical thunderheads seen from my cozy window. The design is a log-cabin block to reinforce "shelter." I used warm skin tones to make the stamped house friendly and inviting, versus cool, gray, storm colors to represent the storm outside. I really enjoyed choosing the fabrics to tell the story of windblown leaves, driving rain, rising water, and ominous clouds. The minimal quilting is meant to emphasize rain and the embroidery mimics meteorological symbols.

Kristin LaFlamme

Letting the Materials Speak

Just as *Machu Picchu* is terraced, I find that the process of making fiber art is multi-tiered as well. Having married an image to a theme, I still have to figure out how to interpret it onto fabric. My work is driven by the desire to experiment with a particular technique or process that is either new to me or is an interesting one that may have carried over from a previous work.

With *Lost City*, I started with painted interfacing, which is a technique I learned in a class taught by Jeanne Raffer Beck. I laid out the colors I wanted to use in the areas I wanted them, but I knew that I needed more detail than the interfacing would provide. I thought about stitching the detail directly onto the piece, but quickly realized that stitching would only provide highlight, rather than the detail I was looking for. Instead, I decided to try making a screen image with my Thermofax machine.

Thermofax machines were originally produced to create copies and overhead transparencies. While its primary use today is to create transfers used in tattoo parlors (thus driving up the cost of used machines), artists have discovered that the Thermofax machine can be used to create a quick and relatively inexpensive stencil suitable for detailed screenprinting. (Read Gerrie's sidebar on Thermofax machines on page 119.) I was challenged by the fact that the machine only makes screens 9 inches (22.9 cm) wide and this was to be a 12-inch (30.5 cm) piece. I ended up splitting the image between two screens and then carefully lined them up to print onto the fabric. The result of this process was to create a screened image 18 inches (45.7 cm) across, which I then cropped to 12 x 12 inches (30.5 x 30.5 cm). I added a bit of machine stitching to create some depth.

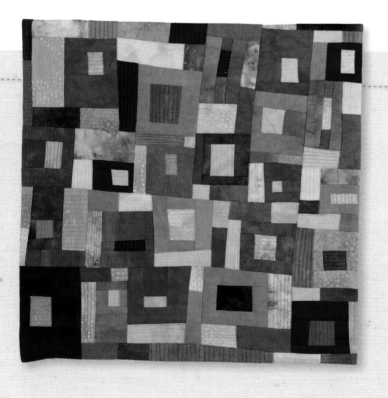

Favela

My comfortable home, my shelter, overlooks the beach of Copacabana in New South Wales, Australia. By contrast, the hills above the "other" Copacabana, in Rio de Janeiro, Brazil, are densely crowded with improvisational, irregular shantytown structures known as "favela," which provide shelter to a significant population. It is a freeform piece, with log-cabin-esque piecing.

Brenda Gael Smith

My Studio

The artist's studio is the place where it all comes together. Whether your creative workspace is a small corner of a den, a dedicated room, your garage, or perhaps a rented space away from home, I think that the studio itself has as much to do with the creative process as it does the challenge, the inspiration, and the materials. It is ultimately the place where we are artists.

My studio has developed slowly over the years to become the wonderful room that it is today. As each of my four children moved out to start their own lives, I moved in to start mine. Tearing down walls to create open space, I have now accumulated a workspace that measures 20 x 30 feet (6.1 x 9.1 m). About a third of my studio is dedicated to wet work.

Rooms for Rent

Bird watching has become one of my favorite outdoor activities. I feed the birds and have started adding nesting boxes around my yard to help attract more birds to my viewing area. I like that I can provide shelter for the birds while they raise their young. I fused several green fabrics to create the background and I added a light-colored area in the lower foreground to give the illusion of a walking path. All the fabrics in the foreground are fused and raw-edge appliquéd. They were cut freehand and free-motion quilted. Black and white paints add shading and highlights.

Terri Stegmiller

The wet area includes a small metal restaurant sink where I mix my dyes, and a screen-printing sink with a spray rinser. I have a large, plastic-covered table where I paint, dye, and print. With shelves above and below for all my various potions, paintbrushes, stamps, and assorted toys, everything is within easy reach.

The room has a slanted ceiling that allowed me to design a large cabinet with lots of drawers and cubbies for books and fabric. I have a design wall made of flannel-covered fiberboard where I am able to design, try out ideas, let unfinished work simmer, and photograph my finished pieces. My sewing table is situated in front of a window with a beautiful view of the Tehachapi Mountains.

Finally...

Lost City was built up layer by layer. As I worked on it I thought about how cultures and civilizations come and go, the new ones often being built on the ruins of the previous. As the work became more personal, I began to think on a more personal level. Our circle of friends and family are just small civilizations, providing shelter and support, defense and welfare, art and culture to the individuals that make up the whole. For me, the Twelves have provided an artistic shelter where I have been able to express myself within the structured confines of a specific challenge. To be associated with eleven talented and nurturing women was liberating. I look forward to the future.

Backpacking... in Rhinestone Heels

I was inspired by some hikers my husband and father-in-law encountered one backpacking trip. While they were hiking along the trail, a woman approached wearing all white, a tennis sweater around her shoulders. She looked like she had just stepped out of the country club. She was followed by a man with a huge pack stacked up above his head. He could barely move with all the stuff he was carrying. We figure the only way he was going to get his wife out backpacking with him was if he carried everything and spared no luxury! This quilt is a blinged-out backpacking shelter for just such a hiker.

Nikki Wheeler

MEETING OTHER TWELVES

Who knew I would be hanging out on a daily basis with a group of artists who live on three different continents? In the age of the Internet, diverse people with common interests often become lifelong friends without ever having met face to face. Yet, each of us Twelves have made real world contacts with each other individually and in small pairings. I met Diane, the founder of the group, at a dye class in Northern California before the Twelves were created. Being from Southern California, I didn't know anyone there, and Diane made sure that I was made to feel at home.

In October 2009, my husband and I were fortunate enough to travel to Paris. I contacted Françoise, who lives in Belgium, hoping somehow we would be able to connect. Imagine how excited I was when she and her husband were able to catch a train into Paris and meet us for dinner, then again the next day for a walk around the Quai Branly Museum. Françoise and I spent our time looking at the patterns and textures of the artwork. I remember thinking at the time how comfortable I felt with her, as if we were old friends.

While in Paris, I received an email that Helen and her husband would be travelling from England and staying with Diane in California on their trip around the world. Helen knew that Diane was planning a luncheon with her local quilting group, but had no idea that she had arranged a surprise by inviting Gerrie, Terry, and me to visit at the same time. Though Terry couldn't make it, Gerrie and I were both able to attend. Helen seemed to be genuinely surprised when I walked into the room and then, when Gerrie arrived, Helen started crying. Everyone talked and shared their work with each other. It was the first time we had seen each other's work in person, and I wish now I could have spent more time with everyone.

When our family was in Portland, Oregon, for a wedding, I was hoping to finally meet Terry and reconnect with Gerrie. Although it was the holiday season and a terrible time of year to ask anyone to take time out from family events, they both found the time to meet up for breakfast. We immediately began talking about our blogs and our art, and didn't let up until I was forced to leave for the airport.

The Twelves have been together now for over two years and there is such a comfort level in the group that I really think we could meet up anywhere, anytime, and just hang out. Although some of the Twelves have yet to meet face to face, we have seen each other's art in person at various venues around the world. I know that when any of us see a group of people gathered around the work of a fellow Twelve, we almost feel as if they are looking at our own work. There is a special bond in being a Twelve.

—Karen Rips

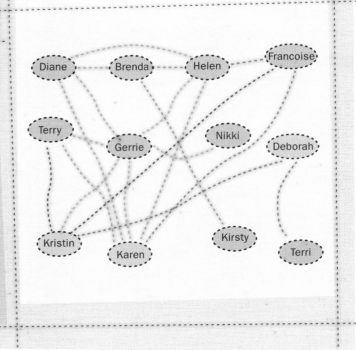

I wanted a theme that encompassed a wide range of interpretations and was different than anything I had seen before in the art quilt world. I am a mathematician by nature, but I knew the theme would be a challenge for some of our other members. Knowing we were up to it, I chose the hardest topic I could think of.

Fractal Tree

Simple Geometry

Change

What Were the Odds

Counting on My Fingers

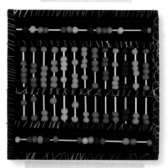

Color Counts

Seven by Twelve

A Malthusian Quilt

By the Numbers

Binary Note #2

First Grade

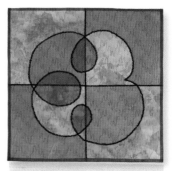

Transcendental Curve

Change

Helen L. Conway

I enjoy puzzling out the construction practicalities with the materials in my hands rather than as a theoretical paper exercise. This is something I inherit from my father, David Conway, who loves to work with wood and widgets and can always be relied on to find a way to make something.

Inspiring Words

How do you find the time? Where do you get your ideas? If I had a penny for every time someone asked me one, or both, of those questions my little mathematics quilt would be bed-sized. I tend to give glib answers to the first: I don't clean, cook, or care for children. I am just organized. I stay up late. But, if I give it some thought—which you have to do when your publisher requires a whole chapter from you— the real answer to both questions is the same.

The Twelve by Twelve schedule gives us two months to make each quilt. While the size of the quilts allows for a relatively quick construction, I need that time to think. My process starts with the challenge word lying fallow in my subconscious. I work at it, words and ideas scrolling beneath the normal running of my daily tasks, like the ticker of breaking news on CNN. I drive, eat, shop, sew, while a stream of words runs across my mind: binary code, hypotenuse, calculus, additions…. I ruminate on them in the bath, in the supermarket queue, even in my courtroom, chewing them over and, when my full concentration is required elsewhere, I swallow them and store them like a cow for later regurgitation and more chewing.

And it is—for my art quilts anyway—always words, not lines or colors, which are the starting point. This is perhaps not surprising given how I came to quilting. A wordsmith,

Fractal Tree

Searching for inspiration, I explored various math concepts and ideas until I happened upon fractals. A fractal is a geometric shape that can be split into parts, each of which is a reduced-size copy of the whole. I took the very basic Y shape and created a tree trunk and limbs out of brown fabric. I added more Y shapes with embroidery floss, using all six strands to begin and reducing to just one strand as the branches expanded. I felt the quilt needed one additional element, so I added a red rectangle inspired by a Chinese chop, and embroidered a Y stitch and the musical sign for "repeat." I think it's a perfect bit of contrast and additional emphasis of the theme.

by profession a lawyer, legal lecturer, and freelance journalist, I dropped down to a three-day week for a six-month period at the beginning of 2006 to find some time to write a novel. My husband seized on the fact that I was at home, rather than in some distant business hotel, to ask me to sew a number of buttons back onto his clothes. The repetitive hand sewing soothed me as an unbidden picture of a serene Amish woman, hand quilting as she sat on her porch, flashed onto my mind. Since I am actually nothing like an Amish woman, serene or otherwise, I Googled quilting and fell down a Lewis Carroll–like rabbit hole and never emerged. I started and could

not stop, and while I achieve moments of fleeting serenity with hand stitching, mostly I remain in a frenzied state of always wanting to stitch one (or nine) more quilts than I can fit into the day. My new blog about writing morphed into a quilting blog, Diane Perin Hock read it, and soon the still-uncompleted novel was in a box and I was a Twelve.

But I never moved fully into left-brain mode. While the patterns I write for traditional quilts—for kits or magazines, for example—are often inspired by examples of African art or by the fabrics themselves, I still feel I design art quilts mostly from that narrow strip of my brain where right and left hemispheres

merge. I have to know: what is this quilt about? What is the story I am telling? To make me willing to allocate time and be able to sustain concentration to create an art quilt, there has to be something I really want to say. I also like my quilts to work hard for their existence—if a quilt is to have three physical layers, then it can also have three layers of meaning—so much the better. And because I am time-challenged, if I can find a way to tell whichever story is elbowing its way out of my brain in a way that involves a new technique I want to try, well, two birds in the hand is better than a bush of ideas, or whatever the saying is.

Simple Geometry

This simple solution to the mathematics theme is constructed from my hand-dyed silks and organza, using them for the background and the geometric forms. My original idea had to do with my ineptness when it comes to numbers and math. I was going to do a portrait of myself with spiky things emerging from my brain. On the right side the colorful spiky things would have had words like color, texture, pattern, etc. On the left side, they would have been blank. It was just too complicated for me to pull off. So I went for keep it simple, stupid!! I had the most angst over making this quilt, but it is one of my favorites. All of the images are fused and then machine-quilted with a simple linear design.

So I take the challenge word—mathematics—and bring it for a walk along a twisty road and see where I can go with it. And sometime later, unexpectedly, when I am barely thinking about it, the idea will gush up more or less fully formed. For *Change* this happened at about 3 a.m. U.K. time, as I was slipping ever further down the sofa waiting for the U.S. news networks to declare Ohio in the 2008 election so that we could finally go to bed knowing history had been made.

I sat, with half-glazed vision, watching the maps changing from red to blue and back as predictions turned to reality, the little CNN line scrolling in my head as on the screen. Votes were being counted. The world was being changed.

People were voting for the first time ever. People counted for the first time. From left field a sudden recollection came of a story my husband had told me. He was in a shop and the person in front of him seemed to be taking an unreasonably long time to complete a simple purchase. He was starting to get irritated when the woman—in her forties he guessed—turned and apologized saying, "I am sorry. I am just learning to count change." Ta da! There it was: a quilt about Obama, and change and voting and counting and zzzzz...it was too late and I fell asleep on the outside. But inside, my mind must still have been ruminating because I woke up knowing just how to make the quilt. Often I do use a sketchbook for ideas but with this one I just went to work.

Making My Workspace Work

I enjoy puzzling out the construction practicalities with the materials in my hands rather than as a theoretical paper exercise. This is something I inherit from my father, David Conway, who loves to work with wood and widgets and can always be relied on to find a way to make something. It seems that the urge to create with textiles and not timber may come more from the side of Marcia, my mother—she is a patient and accurate embroiderer and a recent delve into family history shows a seamstress, a tailor, and at least two sailmakers on her father's side. I am not sure which set of genes should be blamed for my inability to create art without at the same time creating a huge mess of my surroundings!

What Were the Odds?

Maths? Seriously? Then I happened to watch a fascinating documentary that discussed the attraction that human beings have to pattern, order, and sequences. We find it very difficult to accept truly random things. I've noticed this when teaching scrap-quilt classes that require blind selection of fabrics—most quilters just cannot do it! We always want to rearrange. So what about a scrap quilt where the fabrics were randomly selected and yet a pattern resulted? What would be the odds of that? The scale needed to be small to give a true scrap-quilt appearance. Never again will I attempt such folly!

Kirsten Duncan

I do not have a dedicated studio as such but have commandeered the dining room, where I have hidden the chairs under a quilt so I can walk around the table unhindered and get to my cutting board. A rolling set of plastic drawers and an office chair provide an ergonomic L-shaped work area and can be wheeled out and stored in the garage in the event the room needs to be used for formal eating. Because the dining table is too low for me to cut fabric for any period without getting an aching back, Dad and I combined my design skills with his woodworking skills to create a cutting box with mat on top and storage all around, which sits on the table.

The two cabinets in that room are nowhere big enough for stash

Counting on My Fingers

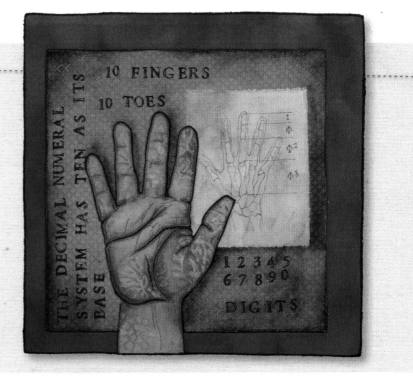

I went looking for the human side of math and didn't have to look far. Right at my ten fingertips was the basis of the decimal number system. The bones in the fingers of the human hand also illustrate a nearly perfect progression of the golden ratio. Imagine finding all that mathematical information just by looking at my hand! My title is, of course, a pun. Of all the tools I use for my work, I rely most on my hands and count on my fingers.

Terry Grant

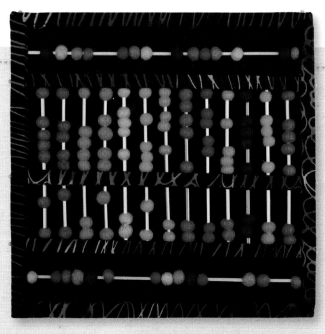

Color Counts

I used the Internet to search for math concepts, and when a site came up about how to count with an abacus, I knew I'd found my topic. The graphic look of the lines and circles of the abacus, and its place in Chinese culture, immediately appealed to me. A typical Chinese abacus has two sections. The top is called "heaven" and the bottom is called "earth." I love that. Each rod represents a decimal place, with the "earth" section representing units of one and the top "heaven" section representing corresponding units of five. I was inspired by Helen's dimensional quilt constructions to try to create a working abacus out of fabric. I covered the balsa wood frame with fabric, slid felted wool beads onto bamboo skewers, and backed the structure with quilted black fabric. This piece not only illustrated "mathematics" but also involved a lot of calculations to get it to fit together!

Diane Perin Hock

containment, so the spare bedroom closet has been commandeered too. When setting up this storage system, I ordered so many boxes that the company representative and I ended up chatting by email! I included some rolling drawers and a folding picnic table (which can be hidden behind the sofa bed) so I can create a sketchbook station that can easily be hidden away when guests come.

But for dyeing, fabric painting, or heat gun work I am banished to a freezing-cold, hideously under-equipped corner of a garage. At the time of writing (just at the end of one of the worst British winters in history) we are hunting for a perfect studio with new house attached before I die of either hypothermia or frustrated creativity.

Seven by Twelve

I wanted to make a quilt inspired by the mathematics small children have to learn in primary school, like the multiplication tables. Thinking of our Twelve by Twelve group, I picked the 12-times table. I screen-printed some of my fabric with this table. I pieced a few blocks, log cabin style. In the center of each block, I wrote the multiples of 12, up to 7 times 12, because this was our seventh challenge. The narrow yellow lines are reminiscent of the Table of Pythagoras.

Françoise JANART

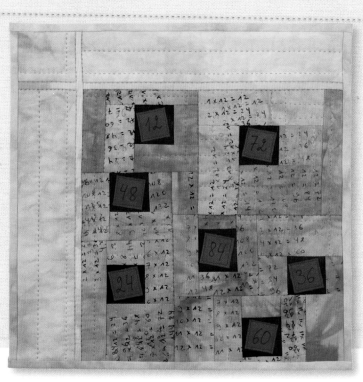

Creating *Change*

All my quilts were created in this makeshift studio, which serves me well. After the burst of late-night inspiration I mentioned a few pages ago, I began to work on *Change*. It is made from fabric backed with a heavy-weight fusible (to give a rigid, supporting background) and finished with the satin-stitch technique I borrowed from fellow Twelve Terri. I then painted two squares of Lutradur, one red and one blue.

The blue squares were then cut into strips, but left intact at the top, leaving a hinge. The red square was cut into two pieces, each 6 x 12 inches (15.2 x 30.5 cm), and each of those was cut into strips, again leaving a hinge along the 12-inch-

A Malthusian Quilt

Charts are basically visual math. My quilt is a chart inspired by economist and demographer Thomas Malthus's 1798 essay, in which he hypothesizes, "Population, when unchecked, increases in a geometric ratio, while subsistence increases only in arithmetic ratio." With numbers from the UN's statistics website, I pieced my chart with feed-sack fabrics. Over these geometric curves charting real and projected population growth are embroidered lines showing the arithmetic growth of major grain yields from 1950 to 2005. The ends hang loose because it is impossible to accurately forecast future grain production or potential breakthroughs. The border is finished with small beads representing rice and corn.

Kristin LaFlamme

long (30.5-cm) side. I sewed the blue strips to the background with the hinge at the top, and each red piece to the background with a hinge at either side so the strips could be woven through each other with as much variation as possible. I find that with hindsight there can often be a connection between one piece of work and another; it's not consciously done but represents a subconscious transfer of ideas. In this case, loose hanging strips had been something I was already using in a large bag I had made for a City and Guilds project (it houses my machine extension table). The free-hanging strips on that bag being in turn inspired by masquerade costumes made by the Egungun tribe. Sadly, that tribe

is from Nigeria, not Kenya, denying me yet another layer of meaning and connection to Obama!

On the red strips I sewed little rolls of unpainted Lutradur to represent both voting papers and the number one from binary code. On the blue strips I sewed pennies in a "cradle" of horizontal and vertical straight stitches. The pennies are arranged in alternating rows of heads and tails—another aspect of change. To get the pennies shiny, I soaked them in a bowl of brown vinegar into which I slugged some table salt. Due to a miraculous chemical combination, the tarnish on the copper amalgam could then be easily rubbed off with a cloth. One particularly rebellious penny liked to wriggle

By the Numbers

I am not a mathematical person, so my idea for the theme Mathematics was to show my frustration with math, and trying over the years to help my kids with their schoolwork. I made a Thermofax screen from my son's homework and then tried out a paper lamination technique. It was fun to work with these methods and kind of sad that, as I was stitching, I couldn't figure out any of the equations!

Karen L. Rips

loose from time to time but it can be slipped back into its perle-thread restraint easily enough.

The quilt—made of monetary change—can be physically changed by re-weaving it to represent the political change that inspired it. I like the idea that the viewer or the gallery owner can be a part of the community change for which Obama seemed to stand, by the way in which they choose to display the quilt. Interestingly the quilt is far more attractive with a balanced mix of blue and red than if one color is allowed to predominate.

This for me also makes my quilt a metaphor for the Twelve by Twelve group as a whole. We have had to form our online community by

Binary Note #2

The Mathematics theme took me on various tangents and I started, if not completed, several quilts. This particular piece is made from the remnants of a failed attempt and with the benefit of insights from a preliminary black-and-white composition. I enjoyed working with bright colors again and the binary code spells out a theme-appropriate word "maths," albeit in Australian English. I used freeform cutting and piecing and machine quilting.

Brenda Gael Smith

weaving small strands of communication, overseas, over months, and over cultural differences. We all have different personalities and priorities. Some of us like to be in control. Some of us defer. Some of us schedule or reveal posts ahead of time. Some of us sneak in at the last minute. Some of us are daring. Some of us play safe. We are all passionate about quilts and committed to the group.

As time has gone on we have come to be able to recognize one another by our works. Yet there are still surprises. Nikki Wheeler chose the theme for this chapter and I confess I was surprised, expecting something more—well, domestic, from this busy, devoted mother of four.

First Grade

When I think of the word "mathematics," my mind doesn't conjure up images of complex algebra or geometry problems, but simple math like addition and subtraction. When I created my Mathematics quilt, I wanted to portray the time in life when we first started learning about math. I used chalkboard fabric for the blackboard and gesso for the chalk, as I didn't want to worry about the chalk rubbing off. The children were created in an abstract style so that the focus would be on the math problem on the blackboard.

Terri Stegmiller

But that was my shameful pre-conception. It turned out that she, and others, were able to integrate into their art complex mathematical theories which simply made my head hurt.

When the possibility of this book arose, this process of revelation and incorporation became more intense. We had to establish parameters for the work with which we were all comfortable, agree on which publisher to approach, agree on the allocation of content, all across continents and time zones. Our relationship to one another changed as we were forced to reveal new concerns, new insecurities, new ambitions, and new talents. We had to learn to compromise, to ensure that one of us was not allowed to predominate to the discomfort of others. It was a source of amazement and gratitude to us that we were able to negotiate the terms of a contract that was acceptable to us all in our diversity—even with the presence of three lawyers in the group.

How did we achieve it? Well, in my view, it was all down to that weaving process. Over the two years, the combining of tidbits of information on our individual websites, round-robin emails via our Yahoo group, side emails between individuals, and even some face-to-face meetings meant that gradually, we built a nest. We fly in and out as our lives permit, with a grand gathering of Twelves fluttering around the blog on our bi-monthly reveal date. Even though the nest is virtual, not even visible to our followers who read the blog and website, it has become a safe place—a place to bring news and worries, to hatch plans, to feed each other with reassurances, praise, or suggestions. High-tech our communication might be, but is that "nest" really such a different place than a wooden quilting frame set up in an Amish kitchen and surrounded by Pennsylvanian neighbors and friends?

Transcendental Curve

Transcendental Curve: a curve that is not an algebraic curve...What? Don't worry—sometimes even I can't get my head around the mathematical principles behind my quilt. The imagery is based on the Fourier series and phase vectors. The idea is that relatively simple sine waves are added together in different phases to form more complex curves. The large image is the wave on the complex plane where it repeats in a cyclical fashion. The quilting lines are the periodic signal of the same wave. This is definitely a case where an artist rendering is much easier to understand than the mathematical explanation!

Nikki Wheeler

ON SKETCHBOOKS AND JOURNALS

Sketchbooks are not just about sketching.

In fact, if the very word "sketch" makes you break out in hives, they will probably not even contain sketches. Think of them as your personal assistant who scurries around behind you collecting and filing the momentary flashes of inspiration that you scatter as you race through life. They are for storing ideas, doodles, word maps, memories, magazine clippings, receipts, records, lists, photos, design ideas, measurement calculations, fabric swatches. Sketches maybe. You may prefer to call them studio journals or design books. It's the doing, not the naming, that counts.

The perfect book does not exist.

Believe me, the dollar store does not carry a folio-sized, Italian leather–bound, lined journal that will fit neatly into your purse and has George Clooney on the cover. So don't let the choice freeze you up. Close your eyes, point at the shelf, and buy the result. Or buy the one you really wish you had randomly pointed at. Or better, buy a range. Treat yourself to a special one. Stuff a bundle of loose scrap pages into an elastic band. Bind your own. Have some for wet media, some for writing in. Move between them. Leave them unfinished. Stick in extra pages when you run out. Theme them. Fill them as the ideas come in no order at all. Just get at least one and use it. And remember: There is no law against stashing sketchbooks.

Does the thought of multiple sketch books make your inner organizer break out into a second dose of hives?

Are you keening, "But how do I index eighteen half-finished sketchbooks?" Well, the brutal answer is that you don't and that is the point. Often the best art comes from an unexpected combination of the slightest of ideas or inspiration sources. Flicking through old books in random order stimulates this. But remember: There is no law against indexing either. You can always use loose papers and file by the Dewey Decimal System if that suits.

Don't be seduced by the books on sketchbook keeping.

There are some excellent ones around. They contain many tips, hints, and lush photographic examples. You should read them all but don't feel compelled to follow them slavishly. A sketchbook is an individual product. It is the reflection of you, your thoughts, your inspirations. Those pictures are there to encourage you to explore your own style, not for you to mimic. There are no Sketchbook Police and no law stipulating how to journal "properly."

Play. Go on. Be a kindergarten kid again.

Finger paint if you like. Scrawl your genius ideas with the fine-motor skills of a three-year-old. Make using the journal a private space where, even if that day does not include time to sew, you validate yourself as an artist with artistic thoughts. Use it on a bus, in the bathroom, in bed before you sleep. Dream of what you might achieve. Above all, begin. Then continue.

—Helen L. Conway

I wanted to choose a theme that incorporated a specific object, to contrast with the themes that were about broad ideas. I think the chairs in various shapes are such interesting design elements. They can also represent moods, styles, and places.

She Sits to Dream

Salvaged Chairs

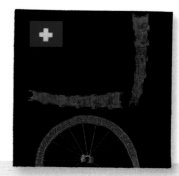

What If You Could Not Get Out of Yours?

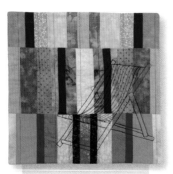

Summer Stripes

Sofia and Martina

The Comfy Chair

Chairs

Birthing Stool

Time Out

Stacked

Rock-A-Bye Chair

Mom's Hideout

Salvaged Chairs

Gerrie Congdon

I walked into the store and saw a stack of old turquoise wooden chairs that were piled three-deep up to the ceiling, seeming to defy gravity. They had the patina of furniture that has seen rigorous use and been around for eons. I fell in love with those chairs, and I have often wondered where they had spent those years of use and abuse.

In Gratitude

When Diane invited me to be one of the Twelves, I almost said no—crazy, but true. The Twelve by Twelve experience has enriched my life in so many ways. I have made new friends who share my passion for creating with cloth. I have enhanced my relationships with friends I knew before we were part of the group.

I often feel like the crazy grandma of the group. I was 69 when the project began. Nikki, the youngest at 36, is younger than my own children. The others range in ages from 39 to 63. Perhaps it is this age range that helped us forge a strong alliance and to produce work that was diverse and interesting.

As we worked together over the course of two years, we became a family, enjoying inside jokes, worrying about a member who seemed to be missing in action and venting our angst over any number of things, knowing the others would be there to understand and send an encouraging word. This was all carried out in our private Yahoo site, giving us a safe place to communicate with friends living far from us. It really was quite remarkable.

And so, I want to start my chapter by thanking Diane for bringing me along on this journey.

She Sits to Dream

For me, chairs represent the idea of slowing down, waiting, and being still. That doesn't necessarily mean being inactive or without purpose. This quilt is a wild, loose, quirky combination of colors, shapes, and textures. When I am still and open, dreams have potential. I really wanted to loosen up for this piece, so I embraced messy edges, drippy paint, and unexpected color combinations. The leaf shapes and stitches further explore the idea of potential growth.

Approaching the Theme

I always have a heightened sense of anticipation as each of the challenges is revealed on our group blog. Not only do I get to see the creations of each member, I also know the next theme will soon be revealed. Sometimes I know immediately what I am going to do and sometimes I agonize over the theme as I did with Mathematics. Argh! I am so math challenged. I quizzed my mathematician husband for some ideas, but they all seemed so complicated to me. The piece that I made, *Simple Geometry* (page 95), was completed the day before the reveal, and is one of my favorites. In fact, Kirsty and I are known for our last-minute productions. I spend a lot of time designing in my head. As the date approaches, I just get to work and make it happen.

When it was Deborah's turn to select the theme, she suggested that we "might want to sit down." I always loved how we used puns and interesting come-ons to introduce our themes. This was her challenge to us:

I'm not sure what it is about chairs but I think they are so interesting and full of design possibilities. I've had this theme in mind for months. I think we've had an interesting variety of themes from literal to abstract and some of us interpret literal themes in abstracts ways as well as the opposite. I'm so eager to see what you all do with this.

It didn't take me long to flash back to some photos I had taken on a visit to a salvage store in Sonoma, California, back in 2005. I had recently bought a nice camera and started a Flickr site. I was on a quest to begin taking photos with an artistic flair and moving beyond photographing people and my dog. I walked into the store and saw a stack of old turquoise wooden chairs that were piled three deep up to the ceiling,

What If You Could Not Get Out of Yours?

In the U.K., assisted suicide is illegal. However, a number of people with terminal illnesses have opted to end their suffering at a clinic called Dignitas in Switzerland, where it is legal. There is much debate about the legal position of those who help others travel to Switzerland. Just before this theme was announced there was a very sad case of a young man made quadriplegic in a sporting accident whose parents assisted his travel. This quilt is a challenge to the viewer to think about her position on this issue and decide for herself what her beliefs are. It is also a reminder to be grateful for the ability we have that allows us to create art. It was made by printing an MRI scan of a spine onto paper-backed organza, cutting it in two and placing it to resemble the frame of a chair, the wheels being embroidered. The red Swiss flag adds a splash of color and context.

Summer Stripes

The Australian summer of 08/09 was the Summer of the French Canvas Stripe. Everywhere I went I saw these beautiful fabrics! It was also a time of reminiscing about our childhood holidays. My brother retrieved an old folding deck chair from the depths of Dad's garage. He sat on it and it collapsed—don't they always? Here is my celebration of the classic canvas deck chair with its distinctive color combinations and always-uncomfortable wooden crossbars. The chair is free-motion machine embroidered.

Kirsten Duncan

seeming to defy gravity. They had the patina of furniture that has seen rigorous use and been around for eons. I fell in love with those chairs, and I have often wondered where they had spent those years of use and abuse.

Out in the salvage yard, I came upon several vignettes that had a chair or two nestled with other architectural pieces, old shutters, iron gates, and pottery. I snapped photos, with the chairs taking center stage.

I had always wanted to use these photos in a fiber collage. The colors of the chairs and their surroundings would provide a very pleasing palette with which to work—earth tones, rusts, and of course the turquoise.

Sofia and Martina

My almost-two-year-old granddaughter, Sofia, had recently gotten to know her almost-two-year-old cousin, Martina, from Ecuador. During a month-long visit, they spent quite a bit of time at my house. I found the two little chairs that my children had when they were young. Each quickly claimed "her" chair and used them for coloring and for meals, as well as posing for photographs. Several days after Martina and her family returned to Ecuador, Sofia came to spend an afternoon with me. When she spied the little chairs, Sofia looked at them somberly, then went over and patted the seat of one and said, "Martina," a bit wistfully. Then she patted the seat of the other and said, "Sofia." Those little chairs are part of her memory of Martina.

Terry Grant

Creating the Quilt

As a fiber artist, I prefer to use fabrics that I have created rather than commercial fabrics. I use many different techniques in my work: hand dyeing, resist dyeing (shibori), discharging (removing the color from fabric), screen-printing, painting, soy wax-resist batik, and photo transfer. I decided to use a variety of these processes in this piece, as I built up layers of a collage.

For screen-printing, I like to use a Thermofax. (See sidebar on page 119 for more information.)

My first task was to isolate the stack of chairs in the photo and create an image that I could then print on fabric. I used photo-imaging software to isolate the chairs from the background and change the artwork to a line drawing. It is best to have an image that is black-and-white, with high contrast.

Once the screen was prepared, my next decision was finding a background fabric for the collage. Since I was going to do a collage of chair images, including printing the actual photos on fabric, I thought that a plain background would be the best solution. Believe me, this was too boring. I started going through my stash of surfaced-designed fabrics. This piece of soy wax batik fabric jumped out at me. The colors were perfect, and I had printed it with a variety of found objects, which seemed fitting.

To create this fabric, I used a piece of hand-dyed cotton that had been dyed by painting with a variety of colors. (I like working with soy wax

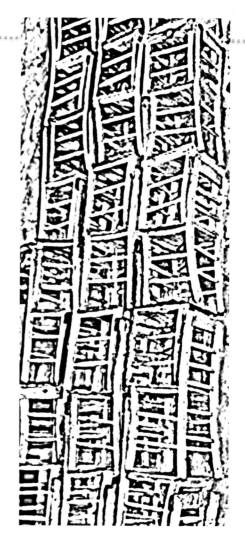

The Comfy Chair

One of my favorite things to do is to curl up in a comfortable chair with a good novel and a cup of coffee or tea. For the Chair theme, I wanted my piece to convey a sense of simple, homey contentment. I drew an inviting armchair and fused fabric onto the polka-dotted background, which I chose because to me there is something cozy about polka dots too. I decided to let the chair "float," to represent the sense of peacefulness and lack of distraction I hope for at those quiet moments. The scene was not complete until I added the book in progress and the steaming mug. I added shading with pastel crayons and detail with machine stitching. I also added small inserts of red fabric in the binding to reinforce the color of the book and mug.

Diane Perin Hock

because it melts at a low temperature and can be removed from the fabric with a hot iron and a washing in hot, sudsy water.) I dipped objects in the soy wax and then stamped the fabric. I used things like potato mashers and other objects that I found in hardware and antique stores. When the wax was dry, I painted the whole cloth with thiox discharge paste mixed with turquoise dye.

Thiox is a product that will strip color from a dyed fabric by breaking the chemical bond. Interestingly, turquoise dye does not discharge so if it is added to the thiox paste, it will dye the fabric where the wax does not resist the dye. This process is very serendipitous because you cannot predict the end result. It is what I love about creating my own cloth.

Chairs

As usual, I had several ideas competing in my head, but the family dining table with its sturdy oak chairs quickly became the strongest one. I embroidered one chair for each member of the family, plus one little chair for the soon-to-arrive grandchild. I thought the tiny chair looked so lonely that I decided it needed some company. Finally, instead of the dining table, I embroidered a house symbol in the center, the same one I used for my Community quilt (*Neighbourhood*, page 45).

Françoise JANART

Here is a word of caution. Working with these chemicals can be hazardous and you need to take proper precautions—working in a well-ventilated area and wearing protective clothing and a respirator are very important. It is not a fashion statement, however.

The washout produced the beautiful piece of fabric that became the background and anchor for this piece. There was nothing left to do but screen-print a stack of chairs. I was very nervous because if it didn't work I would have to start over with another background fabric. I used turquoise paint to echo the color of the original chairs.

My next step was to print the photos on fabric. My printers use pigment-based inks rather than dye-based inks. This means that the fabric does not need special treatment to accept and hold the printed photo. These inks are more archival in that

Birthing Stool

This quilt honors what could be the most important chair of all: the birthing stool. I can't begin to explain how powerful I felt birthing my daughter on one of these, with my husband behind me for support and the midwife and doctor below me—sitting humbly on the floor. For my quilt I sought monumental status with a simple, centered composition. The background is hand-dyed red fabric, discharged using stitching as a resist.

Kristin LaFlamme

they do not fade as easily when exposed to water and sunlight. That being said, I usually use pre-treated and backed fabric. The prints are a little brighter and they are easier to use than trying to back fabric with freezer paper.

I carefully sized each photo and altered them a bit with photo-imaging software. It is good to bump up the saturation of a photo before printing on fabric to get a brighter print. I also printed the stack of chairs on organza.

To create the collage, I began layering and arranging the different elements on the background. The salvage sign was turquoise and blended into the background too much. I changed the color of the sign so that it was rust-colored and a nice complement to the turquoise and echoed some of the color in the background.

Time Out

When I was a child, we had a rocking chair in the living room. Whenever I was hurt physically or emotionally, my mom would hold me and rock me until I was all better. I own this rocking chair now and it still evokes strong memories for me when I look at it.

I wanted a feeling of movement and I accomplished this by printing the image on organza and overlapping it three times. I was really stuck at this point, as I didn't want to take the focus away from the chair, but I didn't want to just frame it in. I remembered a weaving class I took from my friend Ellenina Gaston several years ago, and thought about weaving in the memories I had from my childhood.

Karen L. Rips

Exploring the Twelve Quilts

Now the image looked unbalanced. I decided to make another sign, using a font that looked old and chipped. I used the word "chairs" and printed it on organza in a rusty color.

I was really pleased with the resulting collage and decided no additional ephemera were needed. I fused the elements of the collage in place, which allowed me to create in a more painterly way. A very simple quilting design of vertical and horizontal lines was used to hold the pieces in place.

The reveal was exciting because I knew I had created a really interesting piece. It seems that each reveal gets better than the one preceding. The array of chairs that were revealed on the morning of February 1 was spectacular. I always try to guess who did a piece before I look at the name.

Deborah does carefully created collages of elements fitting the theme. She uses bright and clear colors and loves purple and green. She surprised herself with the colors of her chair piece, but the elements and the hand stitching were unmistakably Deborah's.

Helen makes a social comment in her work, always making the viewer stop and think, as she did with the abstracted wheel chair, with images of the spine as parts of the chair.

About this piece, she said, "With this quilt, I am asking you to consider—if you feel able to bear it—what you would feel if you could not get out of your chair."

Kirsten finds the whimsy in the theme, using hand stitching and a colorful palette. I always enjoy reading about her quilts because she has such a wicked sense of humor. About her chair, she said, "So here, once more, is a quilt from me that owes its existence simply to beautiful colors."

Terry's work is always impeccable and well designed. She enhances commercial fabrics by adding her own elements to the fabric through pencils and stamping with paint. Her color palette is very earthy and is usually in oranges, rusts, and neutrals. Terry is a wonderful

Stacked

This theme brought back memories of when I accompanied my father to screen movies in community halls in rural New Zealand. One of my jobs was to assist with setting out the chairs for the patrons and to stack them up again afterwards. As a carryover of the Mathematics theme, I was inspired by fractals and used software to experiment with different designs and color schemes. I also made *Twelve Chairs*, which can be viewed on my website, but ultimately preferred the graphic simplicity of *Stacked*. These are all commercial cottons with intense linear machine quilting.

Brenda Gael Smith

storyteller and the stories that accompany her work are very compelling. The chairs in her piece were about her granddaughter and a visiting cousin, who was missed after she went home to Ecuador.

Diane's work is often iconographic. She uses simple graphic images to portray the theme. Diane uses color very effectively. She tends to use a bright, clear color palette with strong contrasts that work well with her images.

Françoise is also a surface designer. She dyes her own fabric and often creates patterns with Thermofax screens. She almost always uses blue in her work. She has a style of piecing that is very Zen-like and incorporates symbolism with stitching or paint that conveys a message in a very unaffected manner.

Kristin, like Helen, makes a social statement or selects a topic that is unexpected and quirky, such as the birthing chair. Her statements are very personal to her own life. Her color palette is subtle and she leans to earthy colors. About *Birthing Stool* (page 114), she said, "I can't begin to explain how powerful I felt birthing my daughter on one of these."

Karen, another surface designer, always wows me with her work. It is often ethereal or mysterious. It requires looking at up close to see the details and to discover the meaning. Her chair piece was the most literal of all her work. Her color palette is very sophisticated, like her work.

Brenda's work is instantly recognizable. She always abstracts the theme and distills it down to its essence, as she did with the simple

chair shapes. She dyes her own gorgeous fabric and uses a lot of Japanese-style shibori in her pieces. Her color palette is also bright and clear for the most part.

Terri (with an i) usually does a very literal interpretation of the theme. She often paints a whole cloth image and creates beautiful faces. For her chair, she painted a rocking chair from her childhood and embellished it with beautiful calligraphy. Notice that we both used the word "chair" in similar colors and in the same spot.

Nikki's work can best be described as bits and pieces that come together to make a whole. She often uses tiny bits or slices of fabric to create a quilt. Her work is very textural. You want to reach through the computer screen and touch it! For her chair piece, she hand embroidered with

Rock-A-Bye Chair

When I was a toddler, I received my very own chair; a wonderful wooden rocking chair that was the perfect size for me. I don't remember if I sat in it and rocked with a doll in my arms but I'd like to think I did. I still have this chair today. I took a photo of the chair and manipulated it on the computer to create a black-and-white image. I then played with some image transfer techniques to put the image to fabric. I used a hand-painted cotton duck as the background fabric. I added some hand-written words and some stitching.

Terri Stegmiller

different colors and stitches to reveal a big comfy chair, similar in style to Diane's. They both mentioned finding solace and comfort in their over-stuffed chairs.

Chair, a simple word and a commonplace item, resulted in a very interesting and exciting body of work by the Twelves.

My Studio Space

I am blessed to have most of the basement level of our home devoted to an office and studio. It is a daylight basement with a sliding glass door that opens to a nice little paved patio area. We installed daylight florescent lighting that makes my studio one of the most pleasant places to be during the short, dark days of the Oregon winter.

I have four tables devoted to the different stages of my work. Two tables are on casters and can be moved about. They are both padded. One is devoted to ironing and one is a print table. I also have a cutting table and a table where I have my sewing machines.

There is a small kitchen area that I call my wet studio. It has a sink, counter, storage cabinets, and an opening to the main studio. I have an aluminum table where I do my dyeing.

The office doubles as a play area for my grandchildren. I have a computer, two printers, copier, and Thermofax in this space.

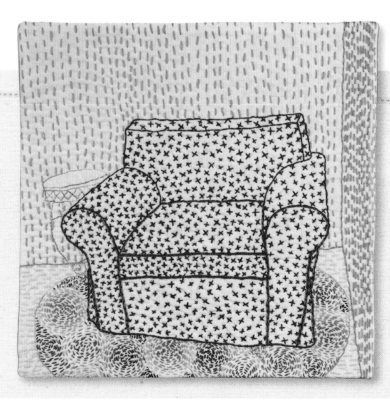

Mom's Hideout

My chair. I rarely actually sit in it, but I have it in the corner of my bedroom and it's all mine. I can lock myself in and have a few moments of quiet, or at least that's the idea and I'm holding onto it. I even make an effort to not cover it with semi-clean clothes. It is there, waiting for me, and I'm grateful for the hope of relaxation it brings. For this quilt, I decided to try something new to me—hand stitching and a pillowcase finish.

Nikki Wheeler

DEMYSTIFYING THE THERMOFAX

A Thermofax, also known as a thermal imaging machine, is used by many fiber artists to print images on fabric. It is faster and more versatile than traditional screen-printing. Once you have made the initial investment in a machine, it is a quick and inexpensive method of generating a screen capable of making hundreds of prints.

To create a screen, you need:
- Thermofax machine
- Carbon-based, black-and-white artwork
- Thermal screen
- Carrier sheet

The machines were once used for making multiple copies from an original that was created with infrared light. With the introduction of the photocopier, these machines languished in basements of schools and office buildings until they were discovered by tattoo artists and surface designers. Because so many tattoo artists want them, they are once again manufactured, but an old model that has been refurbished is more cost effective. A combination of heat, light, and pressure "burns" away the screen backing to produce an image.

Thermal screen is made from polyester mesh backed with plastic film. When carbon-based artwork is placed against the plastic side of the screen and passed through the Thermofax, the plastic backing melts away, resulting in a stencil.

For the artwork, you need to have carbon-based material such as a photocopy made with carbon-based toner, a laser print, carbon-pen drawing, India Ink, etc. I use an older photocopier that uses a carbon-based toner. I love having my old desktop copier sitting next to my Thermofax where I can get instant gratification.

When selecting artwork for a screen, choose images with fine details such as line drawings and text.

Photographs and objects can be scanned into a computer to produce an image and then you can use a photo-imaging program to generate an image suitable for a screen. Images should be positive and black-and-white.

There are various ways of sending the image and the thermal screen through the Thermofax. There are acetate carriers available or you can make a carrier by folding down ¾ inch (1.9 cm) across the top of a white sheet of paper and inserting the top of the screen into the fold.

Once the screen is burned, it is removed from the paper. The screen can be taped to a frame, but since I make odd-sized screens, I tape the edges with duct tape. Using a squeegee and textile paints, thickened dye, discharge media, or adhesive (for metallic foiling), the image can be transferred to fabric and/or paper.

There are several places where you can have a screen made from your original art. You can find a list and other information about Thermofax screen-printing on the blog, www.thermofaxconfidential.blogspot.com.

—Gerrie Congdon

Theme 9: **Window** chosen by: **Gerrie Congdon**

My theme was Window. I love architectural elements. I chose it because it could be taken in so many directions—as a literal window or as a metaphor.

Seeing Through

Ì Chaluim Cille Fuinneog

Eyes to the Soul

Opportunity

Window of Opportunity

Dove in the Window

Beijing

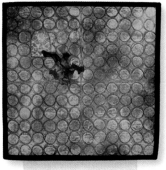

Defenestration

Man's Darkest Side through the Windows of Hope

Introspection

Windows to My Soul

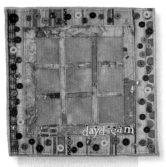

Daydreaming

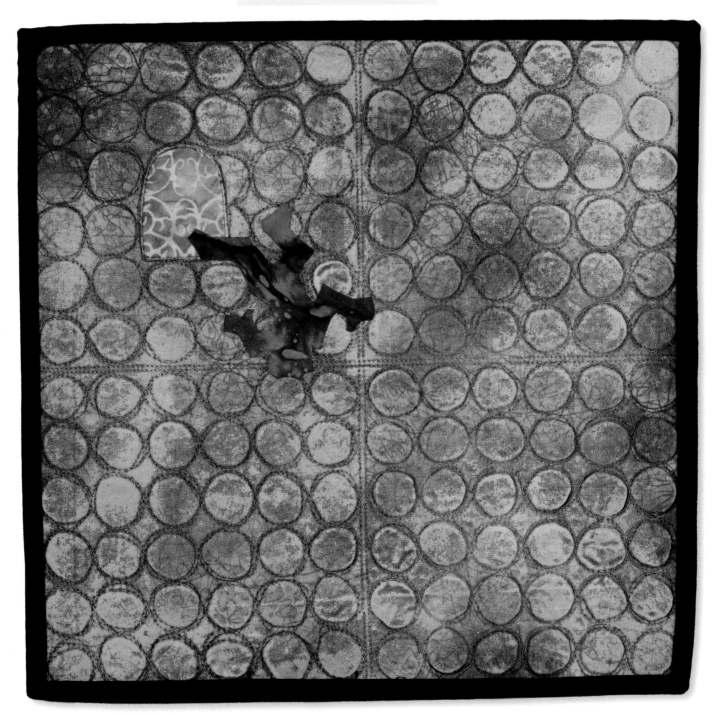

Defenestration

Kristin La Flamme

One advantage to working with a group like Twelve by Twelve is that we can "try on" different techniques or procedures that we learn from each other. Some may fit and become a part of our own artistic toolbox, and others may not, but it is from this kind of experimentation that we can evolve as artists.

Kristin LaFlamme

A Tentative Start

When Diane invited me to join Twelve by Twelve, I had been blogging for two years, had a solo show of my art quilts, and had works juried into various quilt shows in the U.S. and Europe. I may have been on the verge of emerging as a serious artist, but as often happens in life, the view changed. Rather than a many-paned dormer in an atelier, my outlook was to be of the more homely type, watching over the kids from the kitchen window. My formal training, and my career trajectory before marriage, was as a graphic designer—but I am now an army wife. And when Diane contacted me in mid-2007, I was also a geographically single mom. I was flattered when she first invited me to join her art quilt challenge group. But I was also overwhelmed by the idea of adding more to my to-do list. I tend to fill my time as a stay-at-home mom with grand ideas and plans for my own art. Yet I fill that same time with commitments to groups like the local quilt guild or military support group or activities for the kids. However, I had previously met Gerrie at the creative retreat Art Quilt Tahoe, and she encouraged me to join. I had been reading Deborah's blog for nearly a year and she also emailed me, asking wouldn't I join as well—pretty please? Adding fuel to the fire, Brenda, whose blog I read sporadically along with Françoise's, sent email encouragement. Seeing what good company I would be in

Seeing Through

For the Window theme, I explored the idea of transparency. I used organza, other sheer fabrics, and transparent paint to create layers of buildings. I carefully cut window shapes out of some sections so you could see through them to the other structures. Of course, a real city is not constructed in this manner, but I like the idea of building elements on top of each other, each adding to the previous or the next.

Deborah Boschert

(being an avid reader of Terry's and Diane's blogs too) I tentatively wrote back to Diane. She assured me that I could choose to participate only as time allowed.

Diane's generous accommodation proved completely unnecessary, as it turned out that not only would I make the time to meet every challenge, but I often created several quilts as I explored various conceptual avenues. Joining Twelve by Twelve has become an indispensible portal to meet other artists and to be inspired by their methods and thought processes. The group forces me to create art on a regular basis, which keeps me growing and improving. I appreciate seeing others' approaches, as it helps me take in more solutions to any given challenge. In Twelve by Twelve, I've found new contacts and friends. I consider Gerrie to be my "Quilt Mom," since she has been a steady and enthusiastic supporter of my work as long as I've known her. I have come to see Terry as a mentor as well. I have also found peers in the group. In particular, Deborah and I instantly clicked when we met in real life. This came as no surprise to Terry, who had voted Deborah and I, "most likely to have a whole lot in common."

Facing the Next Challenge

Gerrie chose Window as our ninth bimonthly challenge. Though simple on the surface, the theme offered much to consider. Hoping that we would push beyond literal interpretations, Gerrie included the word's etymology, multiple definitions, and several quotations. Right away we had inspirations such as: windows of opportunity, the eyes to the soul, rose windows in cathedrals, windows from a children's TV show, looking in a window, looking out of a window, etc. Our first reactions to the theme seemed to be a mix of excitement with being completely overwhelmed by the possibilities. Terry complained in a pre-reveal post

Ì Chaluim Cille Fuinneog

I selected the Window theme. I thought it could evoke many different ideas, from spiritual to realistic. I often photograph windows. In 2003, I went on a hiking trip in the Scottish Highlands. Iona is a small island in the Inner Hebrides of Scotland that has an important place in the history of Christianity in Scotland and is renowned for its tranquility and natural beauty. *Ì Chaluim Cille* is the Gaelic name for Iona. *Fuinneog* is window in Gaelic. My photo of the ruins with the beautiful stones and the opening looking out on the sea has stayed with me and begged to become a piece of fiber art. I printed the photo on Lutradur that was painted with a digital ground. This treatment gives a bolder, more realistic print. After creating the landscape from some hand-dyed fabrics, I fused the scene together and added quilting to enhance the landscape.

that she loved windows so much she had too many ideas, most of which were too detailed for a 12-inch (30.5 cm) square. I had written in my own sketchbook a few days after the theme was announced, "I feel a bit obligated to do something profound, but Window is just too big." Although difficult at first, it seemed that everyone took the challenge to heart and pushed the theme beyond the expected. Of course, I think by this point in our online relationship, we had all learned that it was nearly impossible to predict what any one of us would conceive. One idea I quickly jotted down was to create something about the easy-to-clean tilting windows we had in Germany

that I miss so much. I also wrote down several traditional quilt blocks that pertained to windows: Cathedral Window, Attic Windows, and Dove in a Window. I went so far as to make a version of the last block using one of my husband's old military uniforms and fiery fabrics as a play on the political terms, "hawks and doves." However, in the final presentation, it was Diane who used the block to its best effect, interpreting her maternal instincts with a sunny, yet sentimental representation of a child leaving the nest, executed in a sensitive mix of traditional quilting and artful embellishment. Her doves are realistically rendered and her geometric windows blue and open. As work-

ing in a group like Twelve by Twelve nurtures self-discovery, Diane has recently realized that pictorial interpretations are what she naturally flocks to and is now making a concerted effort to try more abstract solutions.

Another take on Window were the three versions of eyes as the windows to the soul. Terri used a soft, whimsical painting of a face revealing something captivating deep within the mind's eye of her subject. I always look forward to Helen's pieces because they hinge on her wonderful storytelling—in this case, her quilt uses the eyes to divine that, despite outward appearances, we're not so different on the inside. Brenda often makes use of her dye-

Eyes to the Soul

As I made this quilt there had been a debate in the U.K. about the wearing of the veil by Muslim women. In particular, in my field of law, there was a debate about whether a witness in court could wear one or if it restricted a judge or jury from observing and therefore evaluating a witness's demeanor. Many complaints about Muslim women wearing the veil focus on the "hiding" of the face. Ironically there is an old English proverb, "The eyes are the window to the soul," which is not dissimilar to the Biblical phrase, "The eyes are the light of the body." Is it not possible that by stripping away the (often incorrect) assumptions we make and the prejudices activated on seeing clothing choices, jewelry styles, body shape, or art, and focusing on the eyes only, we come to the truest way of assessing personality? There are many styles of *hijab*—this one includes some embellishments made from discs sold at a belly-dancing costume store.

Helen L. Conway

ing skills in her solutions. I am often amazed at how much variety she can eke out of seemingly simple piecing and fabric dye. Her colorful window quilt makes a striking visual connection between the soul-revealing window of the iris and the literal rose window of a cathedral. Reflecting on the many I had seen in Europe, I too had considered a rose window but got hung up on the Cathedral Window quilt block. Reflecting on my notes, certainly none of the blandly literal ideas in my head held a candle to Brenda's colorful solutions.

Not surprisingly, many of our Window quilts incorporate panes of one sort or another. Sky-blue grids in Deborah's, Kirsten's, and Nikki's quilts promised openings to new horizons. Nikki's textile daydream for the Twelve by Twelve challenge soon became a series of windows for her own personal work, each offering the viewer a fresh outlook through color and texture and opportunities to try different materials and embellishments. Terry also looked at windows as opportunities, though hers were of the abstract, stylistic sort.

I often draw upon my own experience and training as a graphic designer when I am working on my art quilts. Once I have a concept, then I can explore materials and techniques that emphasize or strengthen that concept. Most of us spend the majority of time allotted each challenge thinking about the possibilities. We then may write or draw in sketchbooks, or go directly to fabric to audition an idea. Some solutions come quickly, others are labored over for weeks. Karen says that she likes to look at her photography for inspiration. For Window, she had hoped to repeat the success she felt with her Machu Picchu Shelter piece (*Lost City*, page 79), though really, she mostly liked the picture. One advantage to working with a group like Twelve by Twelve is that we can "try on" different techniques or procedures that we learn from each other. Some may fit and become a part of our own artistic toolbox, and others may not, but it is from this kind of experimentation that we can evolve. Looking at my own body of work, particularly these Twelve by Twelve quilts, I find it difficult to discern a distinct style or look. I believe this is because I approach each quilt as its own entity, often unconnected to what came before it or what will follow. Each one is a new client with a new set of requirements and new possibilities. Each one is an opportunity to try on something different.

Opportunity

Over the past couple of years, my sister, her husband, my brother, my husband, and I have all become self-employed. We have had many conversations about running our businesses and the need to be open to the many opportunities that present themselves. Some opportunities are seemingly small, but lead to bigger things. Some are hard to make out and easy to overlook. Some are bright, clear, and obvious. This quilt doesn't thrill me greatly; it doesn't have an original bone in its body, but it does illustrate that concept rather well and I suppose that makes it something of a success.

Kirsten Duncan

my own space is important too. In college it was a drafting table in the area of the kitchen that would normally be a dining nook. In my first apartment, that same table was as important a piece of furniture as my bed or sofa. Now, I have a dedicated room where I can leave my half-finished projects and return to them without missing (too much of) a beat. We move a lot, but wherever we live my sewing space has my art books and magazines for reference, my sewing table (an old treadle machine base with a top custom-cut by my dad to fit my sewing machine), a desk or table of some sort as a cutting area, and a large piece of batting pinned to the wall on which to stick prospective designs. My room is also the kitschy haven for my ever-growing collection of red

To open a new door or window, so to speak.

My sketchbook is an invaluable tool as I explore various concepts and ideas for each project. Far from art pieces in their own right, my sketchbooks are simply a repository of torn paper, scribbled notes, and hasty sketches. Aliens in the future unearthing my old sketchbooks would not find a window into my life. They are, however, a shorthand to which I can return, sometimes years later, and mine for ideas. Having

Window of Opportunity

When the theme was announced I knew I wanted to use windows in the metaphorical sense. Windows, as a source of light, especially sunlight, are such great symbols for opportunity and hope. There is a phrase that goes, "When God closes a door, He opens a window." Those windows of opportunity keep us going through the hardest times. My invitation to join the Twelve by Twelve group was such a window. I'm so happy that I chose to open that window.

Terry Grant

and white toadstools, which make their way into my work now and then, though not yet into a Twelve by Twelve piece.

For the most part, when contemplating a new art quilt, I usually fill many pages in my sketchbook, writing down word associations, noting visual cues, scribbling possible compositions. However, for the Window challenge, the main consideration that made it into my sketchbook was a small yellow sticky note with a grid of circles, the outline of an arched window and a silhouette of a falling man. The first thing I had thought when Gerrie announced the theme was "defenestration."

Dove in the Window

The Window theme presented so many options that the hardest part was selecting the one I wanted to pursue. I love seeing traditional quilt blocks in art quilts, and decided to use the traditional Dove in the Window block as the focus for this piece. During the period for this challenge, my husband and I were deciding whether to withdraw our daughter from her school to try a less traditional alternative. Given my emotional confusion, I relished the calming process of piecing triangles and squares. My literal brain suggested setting doves on the frame created by the block shapes, but as I worked on them I realized that I'd drawn one bird resting comfortably on her nest, content to stay where she is, and the other dove perched but ready to fly away. Without realizing it, I'd summarized my current situation. The birds were drawn and painted, then fused, and I created a dimensional nest by tacking shredded fabric to the quilt.

Diane Perin Hock

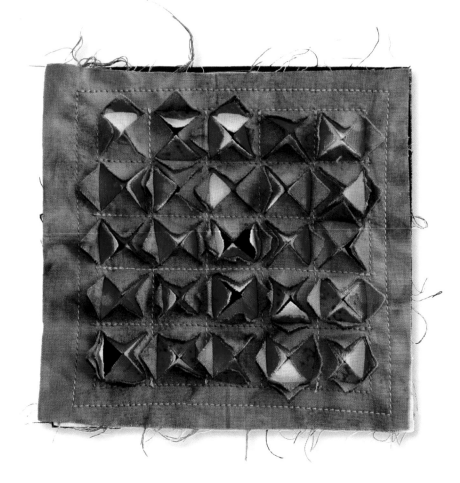

I mulled that idea for a while, hoping that something less gruesome would attract my attention. As mentioned earlier, I thought about my beloved German windows, and contemplated traditional quilt blocks related to windows. Attic Windows and the aforementioned Dove in a Window came to mind first, but Cathedral Windows offered up potential as well, with its folded fabric revealing more color and pattern underneath. Brenda shared a modern sample along those same lines in an exercise she had done for her City & Guilds coursework (at left). It was layers of fabric sewn together in a grid format where she had cut

Beijing

I saw many gorgeous window screens during my travel in China. I particularly loved the simpler ones based on squares and rectangles. They inspired me to draw this grid, which also makes me think a little bit of a log cabin block, courthouse-steps style. I burned two thermal screens from my drawing and I printed the central panel with red, gold, and blue paint. I added red and gold borders, with a touch of blue and green, because these are the colors I keep seeing when I remember Beijing.

Françoise JANART

an X through the top fabrics in each grid "window," opening them up to reveal the blooming colors of the chosen fabrics.

Yet defenestration had a hold on me. It is one of those words that just sounds interesting. Kirsty and Diane both had amusing anecdotes about the word on Reveal Day. Diane and her friends had used it as a silly inside joke after guessing its meaning on a college entrance exam, and it's a favorite "50-cent word" at Kirsty's house. Webster's Dictionary defines defenestration as, "the act of throwing a person or thing out of a window: *the defenestration of the commissioners at Prague.*" In all honesty, it's my enjoyment of the word that drew me in this direction. Well, I enjoy Prague too.

While living in Germany, my husband and I visited Prague several times. We found it to be a richly cosmopolitan city with nearly every structure and square bearing some historical significance. Defenestration pretty much always refers to events in Prague— first in 1419, when resentful Bohemian citizens threw German merchants out the windows of the Town Hall and onto pikes below; and again in 1618, when Bohemians under Habsburg rule threw two Catholic councilors and a secretary from the windows of Hradschin Palace, sparking the Thirty Years' War. There are engravings of these two events that are, to me, the visual depiction of defenestration. I did not want to try to reproduce an existing engraving, but I did want to reference them. I focused in on one detail—a great tool for distilling an idea down to its essence. Given our theme, I concentrated on the bull's-eye windows in one engraving. These medieval windows have thick glass with a bubbly texture, and lots of lead around each circle.

Man's Darkest Side through the Windows of Hope

We visited Hiroshima a few years ago, and it was a very moving experience. The Peace Park is full of tragic and hopeful scenes. One of the sights that struck me the most was this building, the former Promotion Hall, that was at ground zero of the bomb. We were there in winter and this tree was very stark and very fitting with the feelings I had looking at the building. The sides of these trees that faced the blast are still scarred to this day.

Karen L. Rip

Creating the Quilt

How would I convey this sense of thickness, transparency, strong linear forms, and historic time period? I have long admired the works of Linda Kemshall and Deidre Adams, who often paint over their textile works after quilting the layers of fabric. Karen had also employed painting after stitching in her quilt for the Water challenge (*On Top of the World*, page 61). The technique gives an aged, textural, yet homogenous look that I thought would convey my vision. For previous challenges, I had appropriated various styles, from bright, child-like colors for Dandelion (*Löwenzahn und Pusteblume*, page 18) to primitive appliqué for Chocolate (*The Marquise de Coëtlogon*,

page 33) to non-traditional materials for Water (*Water: Sustainer & Destroyer*, page 60).

Painting over my circular stitching with a small foam roller and acrylic textile paint was easy enough, but getting the right combination of

colors proved more difficult. My first try was a dark brown over brick-ish colored fabric. Nice, but not very window-like. My second try was green over a millefiori-patterned brown fabric.

It looked more like glass, but the

Introspection

If the eyes are the window to the soul, and Swedish researchers are correct in finding that iris patterns may give important clues about our personality, then iris recognition security systems and eye-care professionals are collecting an extraordinary inventory. All I know is that photographs taken by my optometrist during this challenge gave me new insight. This piece is made from hand painted shibori with machine quilting, hand stitching, and a zigzag finish.

Brenda Gael Smith

bull's-eye pattern was completely lost. So I completed the quilt with the first fabric and added a bit of the green from the second attempt. However, once done, the brick-like fabric, warm yellow window, and the arch-shaped quilt backed by flame-like marbled fabric looked less window- and more furnace-like. I started over again with a scribbly-looking brown-and-yellow fabric that gave both the dark needed for the window lead and a nice glow needed for the transparent look. I painted a pale yellow over it and left the quilt itself square.

From its origin in the sticky note sketch, my plan was to have a very simple composition. *Man + window + space to fall = defenestration.* In a square format, a strongly off-center

Windows to My Soul

After coming across the saying "windows to the soul," I decided to use this idea for my Window quilt. I love creating faces and soon had a drawing for my quilt. Using templates to create my fabric shapes, I fused the shapes to the quilt background. I lightly penciled the eyes, nose, and lips onto the face fabric and then stitched over the pencil lines. These features were then painted with textile paints. I added a frame around the face to indicate a frame around a pane of glass or a window.

Terri Stegmiller

composition can be very dramatic. I had been inspired by one of my favorite challenge pieces, Diane's *Still Life Without Chocolate* (at left and on page 31), which also uses this device.

It all rested on a suitable "window" background and a simple silhouette representing a falling man. Though I tend not to work quite so graphically as I did for this piece, and I had never painted on fabric after stitching it before, I think it came together quite successfully, though I'd still prefer to have a warm-colored window so the figure looks more like he's falling out the exterior. This was the first challenge in which I incorporated a technique I had never used before. It was an opportunity to

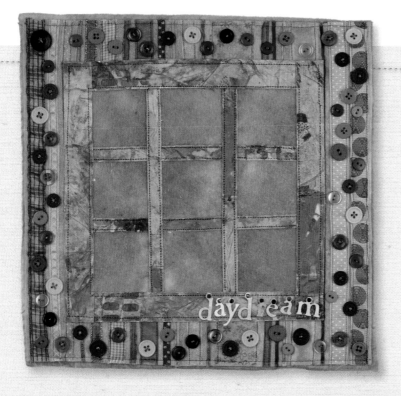

Daydreaming

I often spend my time looking out the windows—admiring the awesome mountains, appreciating the beautiful flowers, or just daydreaming about adventure. So naturally when I think of windows I get a little lost in my thoughts. For this quilt, I wanted to capture the chaos and craziness of my house full of kids and the quiet, peaceful place I can go when I'm gazing out the window. For the background I used dyed wool felt. I then added colorful ribbons. The window frame is made from fabric paper and the panes are thin sheets of mica.

Nikki Wheeler

stretch into new territory, but in no way an uncomfortable one. Because of the small size of our pieces and the comfortable dynamics of our group, Twelve by Twelve has become a place where we can experiment not only without fear of failure but with the knowledge that our eleven sisters in art will be cheering on the process regardless of the actual outcome.

The Twelve by Twelve group itself is an opportunity. Through our themed challenges we are given the chance, as our group description states, "to play, experiment, learn, and grow." We have embraced the challenges—even difficult-sounding ones like Mathematics—and more often than not, created something to be proud of. We are definitely growing in confidence and skill. Why not try an unexpected color combination, more handwork, a new surface design technique, or a different type of fabric? With every challenge we are opening new windows of opportunity. Joining Twelve by Twelve was, for me, like a jump (luckily not a push) out of a window, into unknown territory. Would we work together as a group? Would the themes be interesting? Would we be challenged as individuals? Would it be worth our time? Personally, I can answer with an enthusiastic "yes" to each question, and am very happy to have taken that initial leap.

WORKING IN A SMALL FORMAT

It used to be that "quilt" meant that it had to be large enough to cover a person. However, the quilt has come off the bed and onto the wall, so now we see just as many variations in scale as in other artistic media. Our group chose 12 inches (30.5 cm) square because we too are 12, and because a smallish size would work best for our timeline and desire to try new things. Some of us usually work smaller and many tend to work larger, but we've all found much to like about our format.

Things We Like:

- Small, but not too small
- Fits easily in a sewing machine
- Requires less workspace so it integrates well into small and/or busy households
- Good for working with tiny bits and fiddly embroidery and embellishment techniques that would get lost on a larger work
- Beaded or stitched borders don't take for-ev-ah
- Safe for experimentation without commitment
- The work goes quick, allowing for more exploration of options
- Needs fewer materials, therefore it's easier to work from one's stash
- Good size for simple ideas, intimate views, and more introspective ideas

Things We Don't Like So Much:

- More difficult to create a pleasing composition than with a rectangular (often Golden Mean) format
- Working to a specific size can be tedious
- Elements need more editing—the artist must be discerning
- Doesn't have the expansive significance associated with size
- It's hard to go back to working big

—Kristin La Flamme

Theme 10: **Identity** chosen by: **Helen L. Conway**

To be honest, I forgot it was my turn to pick next and had to decide in a hurry. I asked my husband to help and he suggested the Peloponnesian Wars. By comparison, Identity seemed a topic that was sane, abstract enough to lead to varied interpretations, and reflected the themes that run through my own book collections and professional work.

Palm

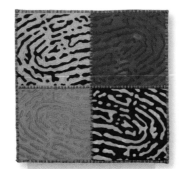

Pop Art Identity

What is the Telephone Code for Kabul?

Face Value

I Am More

Latent Color

Weaving New Threads

Sponsor's Social

Female

Lost & Found at Fromelles

Identity X9

Simply ME

Identity X9

Terri Stegmiller

Each time we reveal our quilts, I'm so surprised at the many ways each artist has interpreted the theme, how they personalize it, how they associate it with themselves, and how unique everyone's work is. For myself, I am learning that there is more to a theme than initially meets the eye, or perhaps the mind.

Terri Stegmiller

Ready for Anything?

By the time we were ready for our tenth challenge, I felt I was ready to tackle just about any concept tossed out. But when Helen declared the theme, I suddenly was very nervous all over again—just as I had been during all the previous challenges. I was beginning to wonder if the nervous anticipation of a new theme would ever go away. I think not.

Identity! How does one portray Identity in visual art? I absorbed the word into my brain and let it percolate for a while. For some of the earlier themes, I found that I would think of an idea and create my quilt. I was only going with my first idea and not giving it any further thought.

Over time, I was beginning to find that thinking about alternative ideas was beneficial. I think I was absorbing some of these creativity processes from some of my fellow Twelves. The exposure to the artistic talent of the other members of the group was beginning to soak in. Reading how each Twelve's thought processes worked with each new theme was very interesting to me. I have always been fascinated to learn how other artists start and execute their work.

During my Identity thought process, Kristin shared a list of identity word associations. These ideas added more information to my mix of thoughts.

Palm

The most basic element of identity might be our names. I took inspiration from the story of Deborah in the Old Testament. Phrases included "under the palm," "hill country," and "into your hands." I used these symbols to create an abstract landscape. I altered the idea of a palm tree to a more graceful, leafy stalk and used a freezer-paper stencil to paint a reverse image of my hand. Since I use my hands to create art, they are an important part of my identity. The title refers to both the palm tree and the palm of my hand.

Deborah Boschert

Kristin's word association list:
Identity theft
Stolen identity
Mistaken identity
Secret identity
Identity card
Lack of identity
Non-entity
Identity crisis
Corporate identity (logos, etc.)
Brand identity

Soon after Kristin shared these notions, Brenda added some ideas about names and their meanings. Your name is a huge part of your identity and while the idea hadn't crossed my mind during my thinking process, I was very interested in the meanings that Brenda shared with us.

Name meanings by Brenda:

Brenda (Teutonic/Old Norse)—flaming sword, firebrand.

Deborah (Hebrew)—bee. Deborah was the Biblical prophetess who summoned Barak to battle against an army of invaders. After the battle she wrote a victory song that is part of the Book of Judges.

Diane (French variant of Diana)—probably derived from an old Indo-European root meaning "heavenly, divine," related to Dyeus/Zeus. Diana was a Roman goddess of the moon, hunting, forests, and childbirth.

Françoise (French)—feminine of Francis, meaning "from France" or "free one."

Gerrie (English/German)—feminine derivative of Gerald. From a Germanic name meaning "rule of the spear," from the elements "ger" (spear) and "wald" (rule). This name was brought to Britain by the Normans.

Helen (English form of the Greek)—light, one who is bright, probably from the Greek "Helene."

Karen (Danish/Norwegian)—short form of the Greek "Katherine"—pure.

Kirsten/Kristin (Scandinavian/German)—variant of Christina/Christiana, "follower of Christ." This was the name of an early, possibly legendary, saint who was tormented by her pagan father. It was also borne by a 17th-century Swedish queen and patron of the arts who gave up her crown in order to become a Roman Catholic.

Nikki (English diminutive)—feminine form of Nicholas; mythological Nike was the goddess of victory.

Terry/Terri (English diminutive)—from the Spanish/Portuguese name

Pop Art Identity

When this challenge was announced, I immediately thought of how our fingerprints are used to identify us. I made some thumbprints with ink on paper, scanned a print, and uploaded it to the computer. I became very intrigued by the patterns created by my thumbprint, and then isolated a portion of the print so as to simplify the pattern. Reverse appliqué with complementary colors created the pop art effect. I reversed the thumbprint for two of the blocks because I liked the additional patterning that was created by this juxtaposition. It was created with hand-dyed fabrics and free-motion quilting.

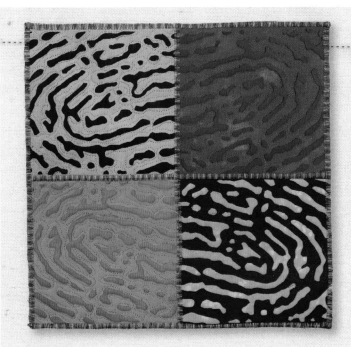

"Teresa." It was first recorded as Therasia, being borne by the Spanish wife of Saint Paulinus of Nola in the fourth century. The meaning is uncertain, but it could be derived from Greek "theros" (summer), or from the name of the Greek island of Therasia.

While thinking on this theme, my first thoughts were of an ID card, such as a driver's license—a little piece of plastic-coated information that describes some basic information about oneself. This card declares my identity to the world and for those who view it or ask for my identification, I feel as if I am baring my soul for all to see. We all have these (okay, maybe not all of us) and are required to use them at times to prove who we are.

I wondered how I would portray an ID card in a quilt. I didn't think it would be too hard. I could use fabrics for the background of the card. I thought about lightly penciling in the text that I wanted on the card and then stitching over the pencil lines. But after thinking about this for a while I decided to keep pondering to see if I could come up with something I liked better, something perhaps a little more personal.

Identifying a Direction

I began thinking along the lines of "me." What identifies me? I thought about me for a period of time and started jotting notes about my identity—who I am, what I do, which roles I play. I added to the list as I came up with words that I felt fit me. This quilt idea was becoming much more exciting for me than the ID card idea. I decided that even though I didn't have a specific vision in my head yet, this was the direction I would go with for my Identity quilt.

I came up with a list of nine distinguishing labels that I could give myself at this point in my life:

What is the Telephone Code for Kabul?

This quilt is about law, travel, and textile art—activities that form a large part of my self-identity. Rolled, photocopied pages from my private journal are encased in a shell of my public-identity documents. These beads are distributed between segments of strips taken from a street map of the area I lived in. Woven around the beads is a fabric strip printed with phone codes for significant places and people in my life. The backstory is that I once represented applicants for political asylum who were interviewed by the U.K.'s Home Office. The authorities often doubted the presented identity of the applicants. Those claiming to be Afghani Pashtun persecuted by the Taliban were suspected of really being Pakistani economic migrants. One illiterate, poverty-stricken, hill-farmer client was required to prove his nationality by quoting the telephone code for Kabul. Given that if his story were true he would never have owned a telephone or had need to call the capital, the unfairness of this question made me think about how we do define and prove our identity. *Helen M Conway*

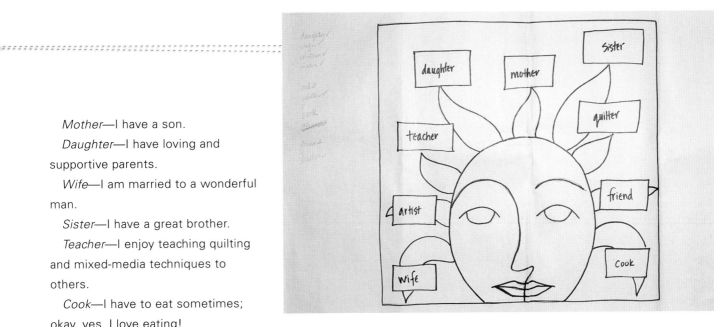

Mother—I have a son.

Daughter—I have loving and supportive parents.

Wife—I am married to a wonderful man.

Sister—I have a great brother.

Teacher—I enjoy teaching quilting and mixed-media techniques to others.

Cook—I have to eat sometimes; okay, yes, I love eating!

Artist—I enjoy creating mixed-media art.

Quilter—I love and enjoy creating quilts.

Friend—I have made many friends through my life and hope that I am considered a friend as well.

I could probably come up with many more identifying labels to give myself, but many of those I didn't consider significant enough to include for this project. I thought about all the labels I could have used from years past, such as student, employee, co-worker, teammate, and many more. I also thought about labels I may have in the future—perhaps grandmother? I decided to focus on the labels I could relate to currently.

A plan started to form in my head on how I could use the nine labels on a quilt. I envisioned a face with crazy hair. In my original sketch, I had drawn rectangles randomly around the face. My thinking was that I'd put the nine identity words in those rectangles or boxes. Somewhere during the creation process, my vision morphed into having the nine words on the crazy spikes of hair. There would be nine hair spikes and each would be stitched or

Face Value

I am going to say this: I loathe this quilt. It is ugly, lazy, and it grates on me. At the time of making it I was going through one of the periods of reassessment that seem to occur regularly through my life. You know the kind—am I still doing the right things? Am I achieving my goals? What are my goals anyway? The ideas for the quilt got too big and complex for my head to cope with and my procrastinating got the better of me, so that this is more of a sketch than a finished piece.

Kirsten Duncan

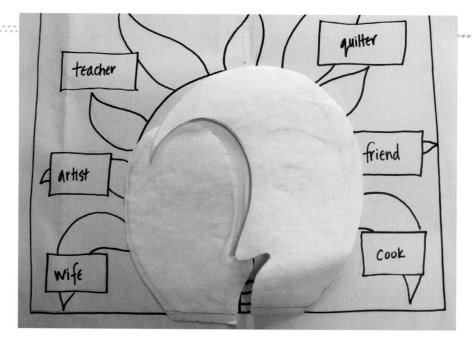

tagged somehow with one of the nine identifying labels I had on my list. I know that at times we all juggle with life's craziness and we are busy beyond all reason. I think the busier we are, the more roles we are trying to play all at the same time. I wanted my quilt image to give the sense that when we are playing many roles at one time, we can become quite crazy and at our wit's end. Hence the crazy and colorful look.

I drew my plan to size on a piece of paper. I keep a roll of newsprint paper in my studio for this purpose; it's my favorite paper to use for final pattern drawings. Once I had tweaked the drawing to my satisfaction, I determined which shapes would be made from templates and which shapes would be created freehand. I made and used templates of the face shape only, which consisted of two separate pieces. My favorite template tool is freezer paper. What a fantastic invention! For the remainder of the shapes, I planned to freehand-cut the spiked hair, lips, and eyes directly from the chosen fabric.

I started looking through my fabric stash to find the fabrics I wanted to use. Once I had my fabrics, I rough-cut them to a slightly larger size than the freezer paper template and applied some fusible web to the wrong side—fusible web, another fantastic invention. I then ironed the freezer paper template to the right sides of the fabrics and cut out the shapes. For the shapes I was cutting freehand, I applied fusible web to the wrong sides of the chosen fabrics and then cut the shapes.

I then placed all the shapes on my quilt background and pressed with my iron to fuse them in place. Next I added the batting and backing fabric layers. All of my Twelve by Twelve quilts (except one) are made

I Am More

I am more than my fingerprints. My DNA is only part of my identity. I am not my eye color, my height, my weight, my Social Security number, or the date of my birth. I am not my secret password or my mother's maiden name. I am a daughter. I am a mother. I am the places I have lived, the people I have loved. I am memory, I am sorrow, I am joy. I am the sum of my parts. I am more.

Terry Grant

with a heavyweight stabilizer as the batting. These products (there are several on the market) give small quilts great support and stability. The only one of my quilts that did not get made with this heavyweight stabilizer was my Passion quilt (*Kitty Love*, page 158). I used a typical quilt batting for that quilt because I wanted the texture it offers.

After creating my quilt sandwich, I quilted the piece and added any other stitched details I envisioned. I utilized the pre-programmed alphabet stitch feature of my sewing machine and stitched the nine identity-label names on the hair spikes. They were stitched in a matching thread, therefore are difficult to read—just

Latent Color

The shapes and lines of fingerprints have intrigued me for a long time, so the fingerprint was a natural choice for the Identity theme. I've had fun using the reverse appliqué technique, and I knew it would work well for this complex image. I scanned a fingerprint photo, then enlarged and printed it. I placed the print over a sandwich made up of a piece of multi-colored, hand-dyed fabric; a piece of white fabric; a piece of batting; and a cotton fabric backing. Sewing through the paper, I stitched on the lines through all layers of the sandwich. When the stitching was done, I tore away the paper to reveal the multi-colored fabric covered with stitched lines. Following my enlarged image, I carefully cut away parts of the colored fabric to reveal white fabric behind, then finished the quilt edges with a facing. I enjoyed this so much that I made a large fingerprint quilt with this same process.

Diane Perin Hock

as it may be difficult to determine which identity role (or roles) I am portraying at any given moment.

Using both black and white textile paints, I added shadows and highlights for dimension. Painting and/or painted details on quilts have become one of the techniques I really enjoy using a lot. (Here's an example on the left.) It can take some practice to learn how much paint to load on your brush and how heavy of a hand to use when you want to add a light shadow to a fiber object, but I am a firm believer in "practice makes perfect."

One of my favorite ways to finish the edges of these smaller quilts is a simple zigzag stitch. I sometimes zigzag once around the edges and

Weaving New Threads

I became a grandmother a few weeks before making this quilt. I was (and still am) absolutely delighted about my new identity. I was overwhelmed and couldn't think of anything else. I chose a picture of me holding the cute little baby and I did a simple line drawing and screen print from it. There had to be a heart on my quilt and then a list of things that I would like to share some day with this little girl. To comply a little more with the theme Identity, the colors are almost the same as in my previous Twelve by Twelve quilt (*Beijing*, page 132).

Françoise JANART

then I stitch a second time around with a longer stitch length to couch down a furry yarn. I like the longer stitch length for the couching so that the yarn doesn't get too covered with the thread. I find the quilts with the couched yarns have a softer appearance.

I was very excited when I finished this quilt. I had it completed at around the halfway point of the two-month period. I initially thought I would struggle more with this theme, but happily I didn't.

Learning and Growing

I've learned a few things about participating in a group like Twelve by Twelve. I find that with each new theme, I explore and research more. When I usually create art, I just sketch something and create from that, or I just start playing with my materials and let the playing lead me to a finished creation. I think that joining this group has allowed me to learn a new way of creating, and that's good. Having several ways of beginning a project can be very beneficial to an artist's skills.

Another thing I have learned from my participation in the group is that when I'm creating for each theme, I get a little narrow-minded and think that many of us will create something similar. But each time we reveal our quilts, I'm so surprised at the many ways each artist has

Sponsor's Social

As an army spouse, I am known only by my sponsor's Social Security number. Everything I do is in the context of my attachment to him. I could literally say, "Hello, my name is [his number]." Since it is inappropriate to publish my husband's Social Security number publicly, the one on the quilt is fabricated. As Terry pointed out that, just as defining my identity with his number tells the world nothing, so does this. The thread ends on the numbers were quilted in opposing directions like the nonsense of a bureaucracy, or as Kirsty commented, "a tantrum-like protest!"

Kristin LaFlamme

interpreted the theme, how they personalize it, how they associate it with themselves, and how unique everyone's work is. For myself, I am learning that there is more to a theme than what initially meets the eye or, perhaps, the mind.

Now, of course we know that on occasion some of us have created quilts that are a bit similar. And when it does happen, it's fun to see each artist's take and method used to create them. On Reveal Day of our Identity quilts, three artists shared their version of fingerprints—Diane, Gerrie, and Terry, as you can see in this chapter.

In the end, we all, perhaps, learned a little bit more about ourselves and our identities. Much more so than if Helen would have gone with the theme her husband suggested to her…the Peloponnesian Wars. The what???

I highly recommend either creating or joining a group like Twelve by Twelve. There are so many benefits. Little did I know this when Diane asked me. I have very much enjoyed the friendships I have developed with all the members, and the artistic inspiration from the group has been beneficial as well. Each woman brings unique vision and thought to

the group, and while not all of us are as vocal as others, we appreciate each other and don't pressure each other with unachievable expectations. Being a member of this group has truly enriched my artistic experiences as well as my life. A major benefit I have gained from these talented ladies is the drive to try and push myself beyond my normal limits. I know that this push will probably always be a work in progress, but I know I'm trying and I think that is what counts.

Female

Gender is the most basic factor governing our identity, which was our tenth theme. Traditionally, females have been characterized as the weaker sex, that is soft, emotional, and ultimately the homebody. None of these attributes are in themselves bad, except when used together to blanket an entire class of people or gender. As women, we all know that most of us are also strong, determined, self-reliant, and many of us choose to be career women. Yet the truth lies in the fact that each of us is a bit of all of the above.

Karen L. Rips

Lost & Found at Fromelles

Around the time of this theme challenge, a field in western France was transformed into a scene from *CSI* as a team of archaeologists and forensic anthropologists began the painstaking task of exhuming and identifying British and Australian World War I soldiers found buried in a mass grave near the village of Fromelles. The 250 bodies recovered from the pits have been reinterred in individual graves in a new military cemetery and, where possible, their identities will be restored using historical, anthropological, archaeological, and DNA data. My quilt features painted fusible webbing and machine quilting, and is embellished with found bottle caps.

Brenda Gael Smith

QUILT FINISHING TECHNIQUES

Just as there are many techniques that a quilter can use to create a quilt, the same is true with finishing one.

While a traditional binding technique is the best choice for a quilt that will be used on a bed or sofa, when it comes to quilts that will be hung on the wall, the sky is the limit. When the Twelves were discussing their various finishing techniques, Deborah stated, "The finishing is another opportunity to add a bit of design or detail."

One of my favorite ways to finish my Twelve by Twelve quilts was to zigzag around all four sides. This stitch can be a satin stitch to completely cover the edge, or you can adjust your stitch length to create a spiky, fun stitch.

To stitch a neat and tidy zigzag or satin finish around your quilt's edges, start by turning your sewing machine needle down in the right-hand swing of the stitch. Move your quilt over to the needle position so that it just touches the needle without pushing it. As you stitch your zigzag, the left hand swing of the stitch will stitch into the quilt and the right hand swing will be along the outer edge of the quilt, but not stitching into the quilt. When you reach a corner, stop with the needle down on the right, swing the quilt around to the next edge and continue your stitching.

I like to further embellish the edge of the quilt by couching a novelty yarn when I zigzag the edges. When doing so, use a long stitch length or too much of your lovely yarn will be covered up.

Brenda used eight different techniques for finishing her quilts, including Terry's satin stitch/zigzag finishing technique. See tutorials for some of Brenda's finishes here:

www.serendipitypatchwork.com.au/alternatives.html

Kristin has finished her quilts with many different techniques as well.

Nikki used some wonderful embellishment items in her quilts, including copper foil tape, beads, and yarn. Karen tends to use a pillowcase finish on everything she makes. Diane likes simple edge finishes, using either traditional bindings, facings, or pillowcase finishes. Gerrie's main edging is a satin-stitched edge and she enjoys using variegated threads. Terry used her covered, perle-cotton edge finish on nearly all of her pieces. See her tutorial at:

www.andsewitgoes.blogspot.com/2007/11/another-beetle-and-little-toot-toot.html

Deborah's method for attaching beads around the edge of a quilt is a simple blanket stitch in which she catches a bead as she takes the stitch at the edge of the quilt. She feels it works best in small sections rather than around the whole quilt.

—Terri Stegmiller

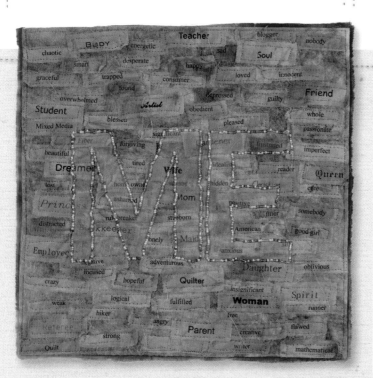

Simply ME

My identity has always been a bit of a struggle. I've never quite fit into any of the categories. I failed the personality tests. When given two words to describe myself I always answered both. Finally, I took a Facebook quiz that summed up my identity struggle: "Walking Contradiction!" Perfect! I finally know who I am and can embrace the craziness.

To create the quilt, I printed all the words I could think of to describe myself on paint-rag fabric. I stitched these down with raw edges on wool felt. I then added the word "ME" with sheer fabric and outlined it with tiny beads.

Nikki Wheeler

Theme 11: **Passion** chosen by: **Kirsten Duncan**

I may have been a little bit mean in my choice of theme! I deliberately chose the challenge of an abstract idea and considered Truth and Spirit before settling on Passion, a favorite concept that I have considered frequently.

Passion Flower Interpretation

Satin Sheets

Together in Division

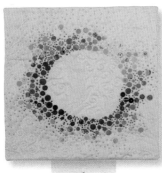

Oh

Passion & Pain

Crime of Passion

Passion and Colours

Lilikoi

Hot Hot Hot

Desire Lines #2: Caliente

Kitty Love

Passion Interrupted

Feature Quilt

Passion & Pain

Terry Grant

Her marriage to painter Diego Rivera was complicated and exhausting. They separated several times, yet they always came back to one another. She said, "There have been two terrible accidents in my life—the trolley and Diego. Diego was, by far, the worst."

The Next Theme

The announcement of each new theme for our group was always exciting. The themes ranged from simple and quite literal, such as Dandelion and Chair, to complex and intriguing, like Community and Identity. Sometimes the idea for my piece popped into my head immediately. Sometimes I had to work my way through several ideas before something really took. When Kirsten announced that the next theme would be Passion, I knew right away that I was in trouble. There are things that I am passionate about, of course, but nothing I could envision addressing in a small quilt. Part of my problem was the power of the word. In my mind passion must not be trivialized. Passion is a word not to be used lightly. As I said in my blog comments, "To say 'I am passionate about cheese,' for example,

strikes me as foolish." I began to seek examples of passion outside myself and considered the fiery passion of the flamenco or the music of Edith Piaf. That is when I realized that a passion for artistic expression is the passion I most identify with.

To represent artistic passion I thought of the Mexican artist Frida Kahlo. I saw her work, in person, at an exhibit in Seattle several years ago and was struck by the power of her images. Then I saw the outstanding movie about her life and learned about the tragedy, pain, and tumultuous relationships that shaped her art. She was seriously injured in a trolley accident as a teenager. The injuries caused her disability and pain for the rest of her life. Her marriage to painter Diego Rivera was complicated and exhausting. They separated several times, yet they

Terry Grant

Passion Flower Interpretation

After several false starts trying to print an image of a passionflower on a large piece of organza, I had to go to Plan B. Sometimes, Plan B turns out better than Plan A ever would have. I took a risk and put together some unusual elements for this image, including fabric printed with coffee cups and bits of text from an Asian newspaper. I added free-motion stitching, hand embroidery, painting, and beads for the final details. Passion has many meanings and interpretations. I think this flower is as complicated and beautiful as the word itself.

Deborah Boschert

always came back to one another. She said, "There have been two terrible accidents in my life—the trolley and Diego. Diego was, by far, the worst." Frida painted many self-portraits, some depicting the pain she lived with, but also many that celebrated the wild beauty of her beloved Mexico and the intensity of her passion for life, for color, for the world in all its splendor and pain.

Frida had entered my consciousness. In 2007, on a trip to Mexico City, I made a special effort to visit the museum that was once her home and housed many of her paintings, her spectacular native clothing, and the tiny bed that imprisoned her as an invalid and which appears in so many of her paintings. And so Frida became my symbol of Passion.

Satin Sheets

This theme was fun, just wondering what direction the others would go with this. I decided to go with a titillating, tongue-in-cheek view of Passion. I cut strips of silk charmeuse that I wove into a pattern on a white silk background to denote a perfectly made bed. I then created three-dimensional petal shapes from painted silk that I had fused to make it stiff and double sided. I made an arrangement of the petals across the piece and attached each one to the quilt with a matching bead in the center. I hoped that I would elicit the idea of satin sheets and rose petals, ready for a night of passion.

Creating the Image

Often, my first step in working on a new design is collecting images for inspiration. I search the Internet and my books, and keep both paper and computer files filled with images. These are not for purposes of copying but to get to know my subject better, and bits from those images begin to coalesce into my own vision.

There are many images of Frida Kahlo and most are almost instantly recognizable, especially the portraits she painted of herself. She is well known for her heavy eyebrows that grew together and for her visible moustache. Frida was very hard on herself in these portraits. Photos taken of her show a softer image, with only a shadow of a mustache and eyebrows that are barely heavier than average. I had no interest in copying exactly any of the images, so I studied as many as I could find and worked on my own image—something that falls somewhere between the harsh self-portrait images and the dreamy photographic images. I made a sketch to work from, combining elements from all the images I had collected of her. I scanned my sketch, simplified and refined the lines in an illustration program, and resized it to work in our 12 x 12-inch (30.5 x 30.5 cm) format. That became my pattern.

Together in Division

I am very interested in people who are passionate about things, including those who practice orthodox or fundamental forms of religion. I am fascinated by how their beliefs affect every aspect of their life. Ironically, the thing that two diametrically opposed groups have most in common is the conviction that their belief system is the only correct one. In this quilt, the black "sides" represent Israel and Palestine and the generations of dispute and disagreement. A map of Jerusalem is cut along the disputed borders. The red represents both passion and the bloodshed that passion has caused on both sides. The embroidered and foiled Dome of the Rock and Western Wall unite the "sides" and straddle the division between them.

Making the Quilt

I have developed a method for working that creates dark outlines and details, and I have used it extensively for making fabric faces. My design process uses a simplified line drawing that allows me to quilt through the face, quilting only the dark "drawing" lines. This gives definition to the face, but keeps it from taking on the aged, wrinkled appearance of quilted flesh. I start by tracing the face onto flesh-colored fabric.

I use a light box, which makes tracing my pattern quite easy. I flip the drawing over on the light box, so I am working from the back, and trace my outline on the wrong side of the fabric with a permanent marker. I cut out the fabric face, cutting away the interior lines. I use a fusing liquid on all the cut edges of my fabric piece and then fuse it to a dark fabric. The dark fabric becomes the lines. The eyes and the mouth are cut from separate fabrics and then fused onto the face, leaving dark lines showing around them as well. Once the face is fused, I use pastel pencils to add shadows, color, and definition to the features. A wash of diluted acrylic medium makes the pastel pencil permanent on the fabric, with little change in the hand of the fabric. I added her hair and the flowers she often wore in her hair in the same way, fusing them to the dark background. A dark outline has become one of my signature design elements and I find my method of allowing the dark fabric

Oh

I always knew my chosen theme would be an abstract concept. I considered Spirit and Courage, but kept coming back to Passion. In spite of the assumptions made by the other Twelves (!), this quilt is actually a celebration of my life's greatest passion, color. When it was finished, I realized the alternate celebration! The circular shape evolved as I worked and, along with my response to beautiful colors, inspired the name of the quilt. The old damask was stretchy and it distorted badly as I sewed; next time I will stabilize it first. This piece has appliquéd felt and fabric dots, Colonial knots, and machine quilting.

Kirsten Duncan

to show between the cut pieces creates a more natural, organic line than does applying a line, with paint or thread, on top of the work.

Frida often dressed in traditional indigenous Mexican clothing. I wanted to portray something similar to a dress in one of the photos that was decorated with an intricate yellow and red woven or embroidered trim. That much hand embroidery was not something I wanted to tackle, so I experimented with some of the embroidery stitches on my sewing machine; the results were not satisfactory. My final solution was to draw the trim bands in my illustration program and print them on treated fabric. The dress was fused in place onto the dark background,

Crime of Passion

I'm a lawyer by profession and an avid reader of mysteries. So it's no wonder that when Kirsten announced the Passion theme, the phrase "crime of passion" came immediately to mind and struck me as the perfect basis of my response. I could just see the mystery novel I wanted to illustrate! I photographed a paperback for the book's size and shape, and then manipulated it with software to create my book's text and imagery. I had a great time writing the back cover's plot summary and press blurbs (and even named the book's main character after our dog!). I fused the book cover onto black fabric, and machine quilted the piece with fingerprint-like shapes in the background to create crime evidence.

Diane Perin Hock

Passion and Colours

Having too many ideas about the burning theme chosen by Kirsten, I did some brainstorming with pen and paper. The words that kept coming were those associated with hot colors. I decided to go in my garden and to take pictures of colorful flowers, and then I dyed lots of fabric trying to get the same colors as in these flowers. The left side of the quilt is a piece of bright-orange fabric that I liked so much I didn't want to cut it up. The right side is a logical follow-up of some scrap quilts I made in the months before.

Françoise JANART

and then the figure was cut out, leaving a narrow dark line all the way around it.

For the background, I chose two fabrics, red (symbolizing passion) and green, using my own sun-printed fabric of ferns and leaves. Several of Frida's self-portraits have backgrounds of verdant jungle foliage. The vertical blocks of red and green also recall the flag of Mexico. I joined the two fabrics with a hand embroidery stitch and added bits of subtle embroidery to the background fabrics, for added texture and interest. Passion, it seemed to me, requires some luxuriant detail.

As Reveal Day drew closer, I found myself worrying a little about my subject choice. Had I played it entirely too safe, and impersonal, by transferring the passion of the theme from myself to a famous figure? One by one the pieces began to appear on the blog. As always, the pieces were as varied as our members—clever, imaginative, and totally unexpected. I found I was not alone in addressing passion in less than revealing, personal terms.

Françoise and Brenda expressed their passions for hot color and sensuous line in their fiery abstract pieces.

Kristin and Deborah both chose to depict the passionflower in quite different, but equally delicate and beautiful ways.

Helen, ever the storyteller, created a commentary on the religious passions that divide the Middle East.

Terri's passion is her beloved cats, which starred in her piece. Her work always makes me think of illustrations for children's books and the cats were brimming with personality.

Nikki's poignant piece was about her role as wife and mother—obligations that require her, for now, to defer many of her passions. And yet she reveals that her motherly role has become a different and equally rewarding passion.

Diane's clever, illustrative work of a book cover made me smile at its clean design and wealth of authentic-looking detail. It also spoke to Diane's passion for reading.

Only Gerrie and Kirsten took on the sexual connotations of passion,

Lilikoi

Since moving to Hawaii nearly two years ago, I have been inspired to design some fabric patterns based on the tropical flowers and plants surrounding me. One of my designs is the *lilikoi*, or passionflower, so it was a natural inspiration. I printed out samples of my fabric via the magic of on-demand printing and then continued expressing my passion for fiber by adding more appliqué, embroidery, and beaded embellishment to the lilikoi flower fabric.

Kristin LaFlamme

and both with a wink and a sense of their characteristic humor. Gerrie's "titillating" (her word) scene of satin sheets and rose petals immediately conjured up images from the cheesiest of romance novels, while Kirsten's big "Oh" left it to the viewer to figure out as she chatted about embroidery stitches and old linens and the technical difficulties of the piece.

My Twelve by Twelve Journey

When I was asked to participate in the Twelve by Twelve project, it sounded like fun but I had no inkling of the real impact it would have on my life. I have been part of the on-line art quilting community for many years and had participated in discussion groups and online challenges and exhibits and this seemed similar to things I had done before and enjoyed, so I joined. Little by little it began to dawn on me that, as these kinds of projects go, this Twelve by Twelve thing was something special. Diane had chosen a diverse and hugely interesting group of women whose personalities soon began to take form through their blog posts and emails as well as their work. I only knew one of the Twelves in real life—Gerrie, who I had first met through her blog and then face-to-face when she moved to Portland, where I live. We have been good friends since. Now I was getting to know 10 more extraordinary women.

2008 and 2009 were difficult times for many people, and my family was no exception. My husband and I had purchased an older house we had hoped to renovate just before the real estate crash and subsequent financial crisis hit. As things began to fall apart, we found ourselves the owners of two houses—one we had hoped to sell and one we had hoped to remodel with the proceeds. We spent many months doing much of the remodeling work ourselves, as well as all the preparations for

Hot Hot Hot

Two of my many passions are travel and art. The theme Passion is hot by nature, which made me think of India, the number-one place I want to visit. It is a land of bright-hot colors, hot spices, and hot weather. Hence, *Hot Hot Hot*. I admire the work of the artist Hundertwasser, and I realized this piece looked a lot like something he would create. So I was pleased to be able to combine these two favorites.

Karen L. Rips

moving and preparing our old house for sale—a sale that didn't materialize. It was a time of almost daily hard physical labor, weariness, and extreme emotional stress. I opted out of most other obligations to focus on the tasks at hand. One diversion I allowed myself was participation in the Twelve by Twelve project.

I found I could calm my anxieties by focusing on planning my next small quilt. I could escape from reality for a few hours here and there by working on my next piece. I especially looked forward to the days when we revealed our new work. It was such a joy to see what each of the group members had created and to read their smart, funny, inspiring stories about the work through

Desire Lines #2: Caliente

This piece reflects my passion for lines and stripes. A dance of intimacy with a scorching palette. In a nod to popular culture, the quilt name is inspired by an episode of the TV show *Brothers & Sisters*, wherein Sarah enjoyed a storeroom tryst with a hot Hispanic accountant named Cal. Techniques included freeform cutting and piecing from commercial and hand-dyed fabrics, with intense linear machine quilting.

Brenda Gael Smith

their blog posts. Reveal Day was a bi-monthly party! I spent those days constantly checking the blog to see the next piece, to read what everyone had written about their piece, to read what everyone wrote about each other's pieces, and to bask in the lovely comments left by our blog visitors. Looking back, I see Twelve by Twelve as a bright thread that meandered through those two difficult years.

I'm still not sure my Frida quilt was the perfect choice for Passion, but I certainly enjoyed working through my tribute to a favorite artist. At one point I admitted, on the blog, that I wasn't really satisfied that it communicated passion and thought that if I were to do it over I might make an extravagant heart, something like the

one I had made several years before. It occurs to me now that the theme word is really only a starting point. Looking back at the twelve Passion pieces, I see that the theme led us down many different roads, none of which was the quintessential expression of the theme, but each one was thoughtful and surprising and ultimately satisfying. Isn't that kind of the way life works? Sometimes we arrive at a different, better place than we thought we were headed for, and sometimes the journey is more meaningful than the destination. This project has been so much more than I ever expected, and has brought me opportunity and joy and wonderful friends. I feel so fortunate and grateful to have shared this journey with my fellow Twelves.

ADAPTING COMMERCIAL FABRICS

Many art quilters, including some of my fellow members of the Twelve by Twelve group, create their own fabrics by dyeing, stamping, printing, and painting plain fabric. I do some of this myself, but I find that I really love the bold graphics of commercially printed fabrics, especially stripes and geometric prints. The problem I have with these fabrics is that while they lend great texture and pattern, they are not always available in the colors that I need, and their "flatness" doesn't allow the dimensional qualities I sometimes want. By combining some of the surface design techniques usually used on plain cloth on these fabrics, I can have the best of both.

Kitty Love

Cats are my favorite pets. They brighten my day and make me laugh with their antics. Pet owners become very passionate about their furry children. The background of my Passion quilt is made from nine wonky heart blocks. They were made with low-contrast fabrics so they wouldn't be the focus. I quilted the entire background before proceeding with the focal design. After drawing it on paper, I transferred the design to the quilt background with stitch. Next I painted with transparent paints so that the background fabric would still show through.

Terri Stegmiller

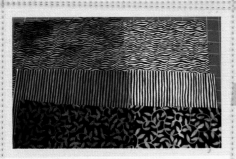

Painting

Using a wash of acrylic-based fabric paint over a printed pattern is a quick and easy way to change the color to exactly the shade I need. I use a variety of brands of paint, which can be mixed. Most leave the fabric soft and don't affect my ability to fuse and stitch them.

Painting black-and-white prints is especially effective. The black is generally unaffected by the wash of color, so there is no need to carefully apply the paint to the white areas only. Sometimes painting over colored prints produces interesting and unexpected results.

The application of fabric paint, mixed and diluted with a little water, changes the hand of the fabric very little. At left are three painted print fabrics, with swatches of the plain versions.

Pastel Pencils

One of my favorite techniques for adding depth and dimension to my work is to use pastel pencil to add highlights and shading. There are several brands of pastel pencil and I use them interchangeably; they are soft and easily blended.

I fuse shapes to a background, usually completing a section at a time. I then use the pencils to give depth and dimension to the elements, adding shadows and highlights. I find the transformation makes such a difference!

When I am satisfied, I make the pastel pencil permanent on the fabric by painting over it with a wash of clear acrylic medium diluted with quite a bit of water. I complete the work with stitching and quilting.

I used both of these techniques extensively in my Twelve by Twelve pieces, including my Dandelion piece (*Weeds Are Flowers Too*, page 16). It included both painted and unpainted fabrics that were then shaded and modulated with pastel pencils.

—Terry Grant

Passion Interrupted

Passion…how I would love to be lost in my passions! For now that longing is more of a dream. The nagging demands of everyday life keep interrupting. Despite my occasional frustration, I know there is light at the end of the tunnel and my time of interrupted passion is only for a season. For now, I will embrace my family and role as a mom with passion, and sneak in time for myself when I can. I used a fiery background of pinks, oranges, and yellows contrasted with the cool purples, blues, and greens of interruption.

Nikki Wheeler

I knew from the beginning that my theme would be the last of the 12 and I felt it would need to somehow sum up the experience. I considered so many ideas, but nothing seemed exactly right—then I woke up in the middle of the night and knew that the simplest, most obvious summation of our themes was simply...Twelve.

Seven Houses Five Trees

The Twelves

12°N 12°W

Midway

Twelfth of Twelve

All Hands

Twelve Quilters

12 Months

Twelve Women

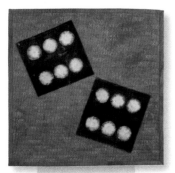

Double Six

Twelve by Twelve: The Board Game

The Kissing Number

Seven Houses Five Trees

Deborah Boschert

In an alternate reality, I can imagine stepping into my Seven Houses Five Trees quilt, except there are 12 little houses, one for each of the artists in our group. It would be easy to just skip over the hillside to visit each other. We could enjoy a cup of coffee, talk about life, and celebrate art.

Deborah Boschert

The Last Challenge

Looking back on the Twelve by Twelve project, I am utterly amazed at the positive impact it made on my art and creative life. What a joy! I am grateful for the supportive community and friendships that developed with the Twelves. They really know me and my art. It has been a delight to grow with them in this process. It was also a new experience to create individual art quilts that were also part of a collaboration. I felt some additional pressure to do my very best work. I tried to apply that pressure carefully and use it to generate new energy and ideas. The Twelve by Twelve project also encouraged my growth as an artist. The discipline of creating work on a regular schedule helped me gain clarity about my own artistic process. I also embraced and refined my favorite techniques and materials. I am very pleased with the quilts in my Twelve by Twelve collection and the experience as a whole continues to inform my art and everyday life.

When Terry announced Twelve as the last theme in our two-year quiltmaking odyssey, I was delighted. It seemed perfect. I didn't realize my Twelve quilt would end up being my favorite of the pieces I created for the project. To create Seven Houses Five Trees, I began by scrolling through ideas of things that come in groups of 12: eggs, disciples, months of the year, doughnuts. None of these felt like ideas I wanted to explore in cloth. I don't usually create art that is so literal, but these ideas didn't even

The Twelves

Good friends are like shooting stars...you don't always see them, but you know they are always there. When Diane asked me to be part of this group, I had no idea that I would garner a close group of virtual friends that I love and admire. When Terry gave us the theme of Twelve, I knew that I wanted to create a piece that would commemorate the group of twelve artists. I searched the Internet for photos that I changed to line drawings with photo-imaging software. I created Thermofax screens and screened images in black ink on the color I most associated with each person. I quilted it with seed stitching, using perle cotton.

Gerrie Congdon

seem like good jumping-off points. That is when I stomped my feet and thought, "How can I possibly create a quilt that doesn't obviously refer to the theme?" Throughout our Twelve by Twelve project, I regularly struggled with how closely to adhere to each different theme.

I had my own expectations about my work and the specifics of each theme, but I also tried to consider the expectations of the rest of the group. Sometimes I worried that my ideas were too predictable and obvious, other times my ideas seemed to barely relate to the theme. Eventually, I had to break free of the self-imposed limitations and remind myself that I need to create art that is truly mine…my stitches, my ideas, my shapes, my layers. For the Twelve theme, I had to take a deep breath and begin to think of 12 in different ways.

Part of my fiber art experience is based in traditional quilting. I began following patterns and piecing blocks in the early 90s. Though I rarely make quilts using those techniques any longer, I still love traditional pieced quilts. I thought it would be fun to return to the beginning of my quilting life at the end of this quilt experience. I wanted to piece a 12-patch block as the background for my quilt. I had a vision of a symmetrical, simple background on which I could do some embellishment, stitching, or collage. Then I realized that quilt blocks don't really come in 12 patches. In fact, over all these months, we'd been creating 12-inch-square (30.5-cm) blocks and yet I couldn't come up with any way to graphically represent the number 12 in a square, symmetrical format. Even our theme mosaics are three quilts across by four quilts down—a rectangle. Sigh.

12°N 12°W

Entering 12°North and 12°West into Google Earth takes you to the hinterlands of Guinea, West Africa, one of the countries plundered for the slave trade. By the close of the 18th century, 40 percent of the world's slave activity was accounted for by slave ships that had voyaged from the docks in Liverpool, where I once worked. Even today, street names stand as testimony to this nefarious history. Rodney Street, known for its conglomeration of medical practice rooms, is named for Baron Rodney, who was a champion of the slave trade. John Hardman also earned his money in the slave trade. Gorée, a bare rock off the Cape Verde Islands, was where slaves were assembled for transport and gave its name to the piazzas near the docks. Roscoe Street is named after William Roscoe, who was the Member of Parliament for Liverpool in 1806 when he cast his vote for abolition. The chain-like fabric was resist dyed in Guinea and the tags are attached with bathroom-plug chain.

Another idea was scrapped. Now what?

The eleven quilts I had created up to this point were all hanging (in that same rectangular format) on the wall in my studio, with one empty spot waiting for my last quilt. I pondered our Twelve by Twelve project and the work I had created. To my amazement, my eleven pieces created a cohesive portfolio of work. They represented my favorite techniques, colors, elements, styles, embellishments, surface design, and themes. If I wanted to round out this body of work, what was missing? The first thing that came to me was the color palette. My first eleven pieces include a lot of blue, green, and other dark colors. I thought I should challenge myself to use more vibrant colors, especially red, which previously shows up in my collection only in tiny bits. I also felt I was missing a landscape. I love to do little graphic landscapes, combining layers of fabric and hand stitching. My Identity and Mathematics quilts (*Palm*, page 136, and *Fractal Tree*, page 94) have landscape elements, but I wanted to explore the landscape concept on its own without trying to add another theme-based motif into it. But wait... the Twelve theme, was I ignoring it all together now?

Midway

At first the theme had me well and truly stumped. Every time I thought about it I came up with same old clichés and none of them inspired me. Then one day I was thinking about my old enemy, Time. I am a dreadful procrastinator and would far prefer that clocks and calendars didn't exist. It occurred to me that there are only two times of day that actually have names instead of just being represented by numbers—midnight and midday (or noon). And, they are special, marking transitions from morning to afternoon and one day to another. Worthy of celebration!

Kirsten Duncan

The Last Quilt

I decided to do a landscape including red and to find a way to make it fit the Twelve theme. I planned to do this by incorporating various elements in groups of 12. I set about pulling fabrics and choosing colors, confident I could focus on the 12 details after I settled on a basic composition. Whew. That's the moment I knew I was moving forward. I had reconciled all the questions in my mind and found a way to respond to the various pulls from different directions. I started to sense potential.

After an ugly start with some upholstery samples, I chose a very simple composition made of red and orange hillsides complemented by a tiny green hill-like shape. The wonky angles emphasize the fact that it's a graphic interpretation of a landscape.

I chose yellow for the sky, thinking that blue was much too predictable. I usually use fusible web when I'm constructing quilts, but for this piece I machine-stitched the base shapes directly to my batting. I used two layers of acrylic felt for batting because I love the stiff, flat, thick, heavy base it provides. Plus, I can do lots of hand embroidery through the felt without bearding. Bearding happens when hand stitching pulls tiny bits of fibers from the batting to the surface of the quilt. Not desirable. Machine stitching just a fraction from the edge of the shapes allows me to emphasize the raw edge and fray it even further for additional textural detail. Since there is no fusible, there is a more dramatic effect when adding hand stitching. The fabric

moves and more texture is created with each stitch, unlike it would be if the fabric was fused down.

After completing the background with those four simple colors and clean shapes, I began adding the details, using Twelve as my mantra. I added the black shapes for focus: seven houses and five trees (for a total of 12). I also added two sets of 12 green brushstrokes in a sweeping curve, echoing the lines of the hillsides. There are also 12 red dots in the sky created with the wrong end of a paintbrush. I enjoyed creating this unique and personal approach to the theme. It's almost like a "seek and find" puzzle. How many ways is Twelve represented on the quilt?

I often create surface design on fabric using acrylic paint. In fact, I

Twelfth of Twelve

Mandalas symbolize wholeness. This twelfth quilt in a series of twelve would complete the group, making it whole. Once I hit on that idea it occurred to me that the parts that make up the mandala design should be elements taken from each of the previous 11 quilts I had made as my part of the Twelve by Twelve project. In a departure from my usual techniques, I digitally collaged elements from each of the first 11 quilts then printed treated fabric on my ink-jet printer to make up the segments of the mandala.

Terry Grant

used paint in 11 of my 12 quilts in this collection. I like graphic, grid-like backgrounds or details. Some of my favorite stamping tools include sequin waste, foam darts, and the mouth of a jar. I guess I'm fond of circles! I like to do several repeats when I stamp images, so in some areas the paint is thick, blobby, and bright, and in others it's faded and barely holding the shape of the image.

A few lines of free-motion machine quilting hold the layers together, but the real artistic stitching is the embroidery. I have a few embroidery motifs I use over and over in my work, including a basic cross-stitch. Literally, just an X. As I was thinking about how to stitch this piece, I

All Hands

Terry's choice of Twelve as the last theme in our first round of challenges was perfect. As many others did also, I wanted to celebrate the connection I had grown to feel with this wonderful group of artists. For an unrelated project, I had been playing with transparency and overlapping different colors of organza. I liked the effect and wanted to use it in this challenge. I settled on hands to represent each of us, then cut and fused organza shapes reaching toward a circle to show our interconnectedness and a common goal. To unify the image, I machine-stitched concentric circles over the top of the quilt and bound it with a strip of organza.

Diane Perin Hock

realized I could combine that X stitch with two straight stitches to form the Roman numeral XII. Light bulb! I added a line of this XII stitch across the red hillside. Apparently, Brenda experienced the same light-bulb moment. Her quilt for this theme also includes stitched XIIs. As they say, "Great minds stitch alike." That is what they say, isn't it?

Another very happy bit of stitching serendipity came in creating the binding for *Seven Houses Five Trees*. I added a fused blue binding that tied in some of the colors from the paint and the embroidery, but it seemed too bold. I decided to tone it down by hand-stitching over the binding in colors that would match the design of the background of the

Twelve Quilters

The dark blue sign is my interpretation of the Chinese character for 12. The 12 little red shapes represent the members of our Twelve by Twelve group, scattered around the world: eight in the U.S., two in Australia, one in the U.K., and one in Belgium. I also added 12 cross-stitches, which are almost connected. As a final touch, there are twelve tiny beads all together in the upper right corner, as one day we hope to be able to gather in real life. The piece is quilted by hand.

Françoise JANART

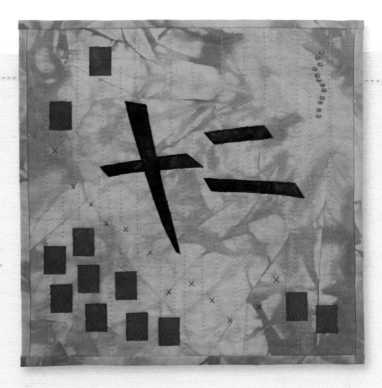

quilt. Red in the red hill sections, yellow in the yellow sky sections, and so on. The stitches are just far enough apart so that the binding color peeks through, but the stitching helps continue the design to the edge of the composition. It was quite time-consuming and I am still searching for the perfect thimble, but I am thrilled with the effect.

The Final Reveal Day

This was great fun as usual. We finished our collaboration with a creative and colorful bang! Six of the 12 quilts refer specifically to our group or our quilts. Gerrie created a grid of our faces. Terry pieced a kaleidoscope from each of her eleven earlier works. Diane layered 12 hands for her quilt. Françoise created a map-like piece representing each of our homes. Karen's quilt includes 12 tall, thin, golden female figures. Terri's piece incorporates each of our names and the themes we chose.

Others incorporated Twelve in insightful ways. Surprisingly, or maybe not, none of us chose a predictable representation. Kristin focused on her husband's 12-month deployment to Iraq. Brenda created

12 Months

After struggling with ideas for Twelve, I had an eleventh-hour epiphany. Twelve months... the length of a deployment. At the time, my husband was due back from Iraq so it was apropos. Twelve horizontal strips of fabric (mostly from his uniforms) represent the months. The vertical quilting indicates the days. Although it is not specifically a narrative, the fabrics and colors move from having the best intentions at the beginning, to the darker, tired feeling one has towards the end of a long separation. The 365th day, however, is marked with the open heart with which we welcome Daddy back. *Kristin LaFlamme*

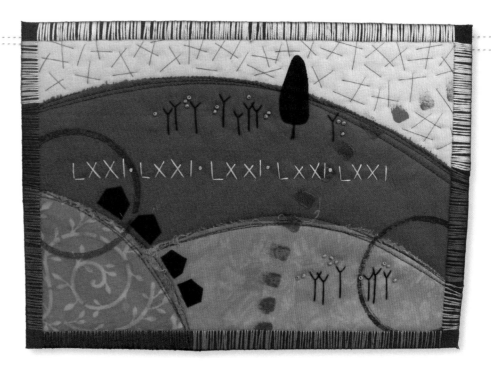

a lucky roll of double sixes on dice. Kirsten expressed her two favorite times of the day: midnight and midday (12 o'clock). Nikki found an interesting math concept relating to 12. Helen (as usual) found an amazing way to create a quilt about an issue close to her heart by focusing on 12°N longitude and 12°W latitude.

One of the biggest pleasures on our Twelve by Twelve blog is the comments that fly about on Reveal Day. It certainly feels good to read so many thoughtful, kind compliments about my work, especially from other artists who I respect so much. Gerrie was the first to comment on *Seven Houses Five Trees*, saying she loved it and noting that

the hand stitching was "fabulous." Kirsten went on to say she wanted to hang it on a wall in her home. Gerrie commented back to make sure everyone knew she loved my quilt more than Kirsten and a friendly match was scheduled to duke it out. I was flattered and humored by

this exchange. Since Gerrie's 71st birthday was shortly after the Twelve reveal, it seemed appropriate to make a little landscape as a gift for her. I substituted the XII stitches from my theme quilt with LXXI for Gerrie's birthday. I titled it *Hillside Celebration*.

Twelve Women

Twelve Women celebrates us, our friendships, and our future endeavors. It is the twelfth in the series, and I wanted to salute our accomplishments. Thank you, Diane, for starting this group, and thank you all for being the strong, creative women that you (we) are.

Karen L. Rips

Still excited by bright graphic landscapes, I embraced the design for another project. A local group of art quilters issues a challenge every now and then. A few years back, we all decided to enter the "large appliqué" category at the Dallas Quilt Show. The show stipulates that quilts in the large category be at least 72 inches (182.8 cm) on one side, but doesn't mention the measurement for the other sides.

Aha! We all created tall, skinny quilts measuring about 17 x 72 inches (43.2 x 182.8 cm). We did vertical compositions, because who wants to sew a sleeve on a 72-inch wide quilt?! Not I. Our tall skinny collection was so successful that we decided to do another round— this time, horizontal. (Sewing the sleeve…drat!) A landscape seemed like the perfect horizontal subject matter and I returned to the clear,

solid colors, paint, stitching, and tiny black houses and trees for this much larger work.

My Twelve by Twelve quilts continue to inform my work. Our group is continuing with a new set of challenges we're calling Colorplay. There are bits of fabric and new ideas strewn about my studio at the moment. I am very lucky to have a space in our home to explore my creative spirit. When we moved to

Double Six

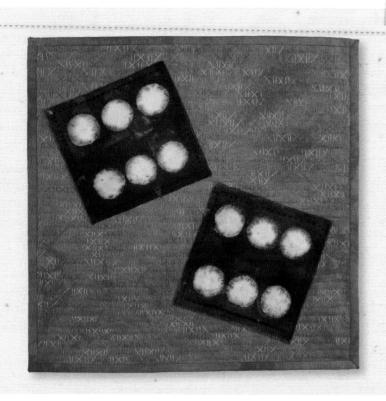

I'm no gambler, but a double-six in dice is often associated with good fortune. It has been my good fortune to be part of the Twelve by Twelve Collaborative Art Quilt Project and I am supremely grateful for the friendship, support, and creative encouragement offered by my fellow Twelves. After first experimenting with itajame shibori (using clamped 20-cent Australian coins as resists), with mixed success, I made the distinct dot shapes using a commercial batik resist medium overdyed in black. The dice are appliquéd onto a hand-dyed background. It is hand quilted with variegated thread using a Roman numeral 12 (XII) motif.

Brenda Gael Smith

Twelve by Twelve: The Board Game

Twelve o'clock? Twelve artists? Twelve themes? Hmm! My sketches started with the vision of a clock face. I divided the circle into twelve sections. In each section I embroidered the corresponding name and theme. I penciled the numbers 1–12 around the circle and then free-motion zigzag-stitched over the pencil marks. At some point, the two clock hands became one hand—a single pointer or spinner. The more I worked on my quilt, the more it resembled a piece from a board game. My husband helped me attach the pointer so that it would spin. Doesn't this look like a fun game?

Terri Stegmiller

of creative clutter!") Recently, I put the table on risers so I can stand as I work. There is also a closet that is only just barely what you might call organized. My red couch is perfect for sitting to do embroidery. All is right with the world when I charge up my iPhone and load it with interesting podcasts and begin stitching.

In an alternate reality, I can imagine stepping into my *Seven Houses Five Trees* quilt, except there are 12 little houses, one for each of the artists in our group. It would be easy to just skip over the hillside to visit each other. We could enjoy a cup of coffee, talk about life, and celebrate art. That may be a dream, but I am confident we will find a way to cross paths in real life. I'm looking forward to that day.

Texas, we decided to turn what would have been an office into my studio. There is a small sewing area that works just fine, since my art is generally fairly small. My ironing board is next to my design wall and a large table sits right in the middle of the room. It's big enough for auditioning fabrics, cutting, painting, and stacking important books and magazines waiting attention. (That's a creative way of saying, "It's full

The Kissing Number

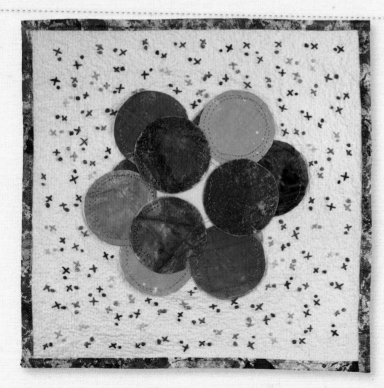

Twelve is the "kissing number" in the third dimension. What? The kissing number is the number of spheres of the same diameter that can touch or "kiss" a center sphere at the same time. Basically, if you have one ball, 12 other balls of the same size can touch it at the same time without crowding anyone out. A rather interesting concept in light of all the "12s" in history, religion, and society.

I took the geometric approach to depicting the kissing number and used 12 colored circles surrounding a single white circle. I then added XO with embroidery floss, 12 sets of 12, in 12 different colors.

Nikki Wheeler

LOOKING BACK

Following the Community theme, we had a discussion about whether we could re-do a quilt after the reveal. Diane admitted she was disappointed with her quilt. We sympathized with her frustration, but ultimately agreed Reveal Day is the end of the theme. We felt that our Twelve by Twelve project was more about the process and commitment than about specifically successful pieces. Embracing the less successful pieces and being willing to share them made for a richer overall experience.

The Twelves have a variety of feelings about why their least favorite quilts didn't work. Some knew the quilt wasn't coming together, but didn't have time to start over. Karen commented about her Community quilt (*Similar Differences*, page 47), "I didn't like it, but pushed on trying to make it work, and ended up unhappy with the piece." Diane said about her Community quilt (*All Together Now*, page 44) "Each time I see it, I cringe at the colors and jumbly design and wish I'd discarded it and started over."

In other situations, the artist felt good about the quilt on Reveal Day, but thought it lost impact over time. Terry said about her Window piece (*Window of Opportunity*, page 126), "I was making small squares at the time and this was an outgrowth of that. The squares quickly ran their course in my work and I moved on. Now when I look at it, I just think it isn't very interesting." Brenda has a similar attitude about her Mathematics quilt (*Binary Note #2*, page 102). "The hidden meaning of the binary code now seems overly cryptic." Kristin was initially pleased with her Water quilt (*New World*, page 57) but says, "It hasn't held up to the test of time. It's kind of shrinking and just looks meh."

Technical problems plagued some of our quilts. Imagined transfers didn't turn out as anticipated. Batting, thread, and sewing machines misbehaved. Sometimes we tried to communicate a particular idea, but were unable to make the visuals match the meaning. I experienced this struggle with my Community piece (*Attached Disconnected*, below and page 40). I like the embellishments that represent connections, but everything else is weak.

Ultimately, though, we are each pleased with our collections. I think we agree that they represent a greater accomplishment and journey than simply standing alone as small art quilts.

—Deborah Boschert

Artist Profiles

Deborah Boschert

I've always been a crafty girl. As a kid I made Shrinky Dinks® and stained-glass sun catchers that baked in the oven. I even took metalsmithing and ceramics classes in college. All those artistic explorations eventually led me to fabric, fiber art, and art quilting. I am always thrilled to stitch materials and fibers together to create the images and ideas in my mind. I create art quilts, fabric collage, and other bits of arty goodness. My favorite techniques include fused appliqué, surface design, improvisational hand embroidery, and unusual embellishments. I also love teaching workshops, creating self-published zines and connecting with other artists. My work has appeared in several magazines, juried quilt shows, and galleries. I recently moved from Texas to Annapolis, Maryland, with my husband Jeff, our children Claire and Benjamin, and our dog Lincoln. Living a creative life is about much more than just art quilts. I enjoy exploring the world with my family, embracing new experiences, lattes with friends, and baking brownies.

Blog: www.deborahsjournal.blogspot.com
Website: www.deborahsstudio.com

Gerrie Congdon

I live in Portland, Oregon, with my husband, Steve, and our Labradoodle, Scooter. I have had an eclectic career life after graduating from Cornell University's College of Human Ecology and earning an MS in Clothing and Textiles from Penn State. I am a lifelong textile addict. I have been sewing clothing and items for my home since I can remember. But quilting? I tried it once in the 1970s and walked away. It was much too tedious and labor intensive for me.

When I retired 10 years ago, I had a desire to let the inner artist out. I discovered art quilting. I found I could continue my addiction to fabric, not worry about points and matching seams, and the end result was a beautiful work of art.

I love working in the abstract and am greatly influenced by elements from nature. My work is often collaged and fused, as I love playing with shapes and colors in a painterly way. I often dye my own fabric and love experimenting with surface design such as screen printing, painting, stenciling, and foiling. There is a new term for this; we call it *slow cloth.*

Website/Blog: www.gericondesigns.com

Helen L. Conway

I am a lawyer living in the North West of England. I discovered quilting in 2006 when my husband seized an opportunity between my business trips and presented me with a pile of buttons to sew back onto his shirts. I found the hand stitching de-stressing and an image of an Amish woman peacefully quilting floated into my mind. I Googled "quilting," fell down a rabbit hole into the wonderful world of textiles and never came back up. My neat and tidy husband now has a house covered with thread and probably wishes he had just bought new clothes.

I quickly discovered that I am constitutionally incapable of sticking to a traditional block, matching points, or following someone else's pattern. I love to improvise, to design, to write about quilting, and to learn. At the time of writing, I feel I am still striving towards a distinctive personal style, am enthused by how many different things there are to try, and frustrated by the lack of time to do them all today. I am eternally grateful for the friendship and sense of belonging that this Twelve by Twelve group and the wider quilting community have gifted me.

Blog: www.downthewell.blogspot.com
Website: www.helenconwaydesign.com

Kirsten Duncan

I learned to sew as a four-year-old, patiently taught hand sewing and embroidery by my mother, who made our clothing, curtains, and soft furnishings; spun and dyed wool; and potato-printed designs on my dresses. My parents encouraged creativity and artistic endeavor in me and my brother and sister. My memories are full of trips to fabric stores and weekends spent rummaging through the cupboards for buttons and scraps of cloth for various projects. I was making my own clothes on the sewing machine by the age of ten and eventually sewed my wedding dress completely by hand (romantic fool!).

I have a need to be making something at all times. Color is my primary inspiration and absolute passion. Fortunately, my eternally patient husband, Peter, and our children, Clancy and Alexandra, indulge my obsessions and live with the lint. And our beautiful boy, James, is always with me, too.

Blog: www.pompomrouge.wordpress.com
Website: www.pompomrouge.com

Terry Grant

I live just outside Portland, Oregon, with my husband. I have been sewing, drawing, and painting since I was a child. I earned a degree in art and concentrated my energy on painting and printmaking. It wasn't until I saw a group of beautiful quilts that it occurred to me that my love of art and of textiles and sewing could be combined. I have never looked back!

I am mostly retired from my career in graphic design and spend most of my days enjoying my family, working in my studio, or writing. I have had several articles published in quilting magazines and am an avid blogger. I have been an active member of a variety of online quilting communities since the early 1990s, and feel the Twelve by Twelve project has been the most challenging and satisfying of them all.

Blog: www.andsewitgoes.blogspot.com

Diane Perin Hock

I live and play with fabric in the wine country of Healdsburg, California. A lawyer by profession and an avid reader at all times, I relax the left side of my brain by immersing it in color, pattern, and the joy of creating visual and tactile art. I use a variety of techniques, especially piecing, machine appliqué, fusing, fabric painting, dyeing, and machine quilting, and I'm always game to learn new ones. The sense of support and inspiration from a quilting community is important to me, as evidenced by my founding the Artful Quilters Blog Ring online and this Twelve by Twelve challenge group. I reside with my husband, daughter, a rambunctious black Lab, and two cats, and dream of adding a long-arm quilting machine to the family some day. You can read more of my writing about quilting and life on my blog.

Blog: www.goingtopieces.blogspot.com

Françoise Jamart

I've always liked to draw and to do crafts, but oddly enough, I chose to study mathematics at the university. In the 1980s, I spent a few years in California with my husband and my first two children. That's where I saw quilts for the first time and I decided I wanted to be a quilter. I was hooked.

We've now been living in Belgium for about twenty years. We have three children, a beautiful granddaughter, and a crazy dog.

I have a passion for color and texture. I dye and print most of my fabrics and I like to mix hand and machine stitching in my work. I love Japan and its traditional culture and arts. I read a lot, in French and in English. I also enjoy cooking, gardening, and sailing.

Blog: http://www.creatilfun.blogspot.com

Kristin La Flamme

Though originally from Los Angeles, California, I was living in Germany when I joined Twelve by Twelve. For now, I reside in Hawaii with my husband, two children, and our well-traveled cat.

The women in my husband's family are quilters, and since my mother had taught me to knit, crochet, and sew at an early age, it didn't take much to lure me. I have a BFA in Graphic Design, but after marrying into the military and moving abroad, it was difficult to maintain my career. It wasn't long before my creative eye turned towards the tactile allure of, first, traditional quilting, then art quilting.

The mosaic of hues, textures, and shapes to tell a fabric story in patchwork appeals to the graphic designer in me that enjoyed the combining of color, text, and imagery to communicate for a client. Although I utilize the sewing machine for much of my work, I also find that my more recent quilts have begun to incorporate many of the hand skills my mother taught me years ago.

Website/Blog: www.kristinlaflamme.com

Karen Rips

I am a native California girl currently living in Thousand Oaks with my husband, Ted. Together, we raised four children. As they started moving out, I quickly filled our empty nest by incorporating their rooms into the great big studio I now work in.

I was a neonatal nurse for twenty-five years, and retired to start my life in fiber art. It didn't take long to discover that this art form was not only stress relieving, but liberating as well. Today, my need to create fiber art is as important as breathing. I make art as a way of expressing my perception of the world around me, feeling the energy of having created something that has never existed before. Fiber is my medium of choice because it is tactile, easily manipulated, and can be altered in many different ways.

I create my own fabric using a variety of surface design techniques and then experiment to bring the piece alive, often by incorporating ideas and elements from previous creations. Tactile elements are important in my work because they give the piece even more reason to get up close and look at the art.

Blog: www.fiberartmusings.blogspot.com
Website: www.karenrips.com

Brenda Gael Smith

I learned to sew by a kind of osmosis, watching and helping my resourceful and talented mother. I made my first quilt when I was at university, to keep warm in student houses as I studied politics and law, but did not return to quiltmaking until sixteen years later. Emerging from the fog of a protracted and demanding business transaction in 2000, I made a baby quilt for a friend. What serendipity! Patchwork, quilting, and textiles have since developed into a compelling and rewarding avocation. In a personal "sea change," I traded my city law office for a studio overlooking the ocean at Copacabana, Australia, where I design, create, and write. My preferred medium is freeform piecing with my own hand-dyed fabrics but I'll try most techniques at least once. I also share the joys of color and quiltmaking through teaching.

Website/Blog:
www.serendipitypatchwork.com.au
www.brendagaelsmith.com

Terri Stegmiller

I have been creating art of various types for as long as I can remember. My current focus and passion is in mixed-media textiles, specifically art quilting. Texture and color are very exciting to me. I find that I'm drawn to creating female faces and flowers. I also enjoy cats and birds and love to portray them in my work as well.

I have no formal art education. My education has been achieved through my experience and by continued practice, or what I prefer to call "play time." I love the challenge of learning a new technique or process and making it work for my needs. I live in Mandan, North Dakota, with my husband and cats. I have been blessed with one son. My hobbies include flower gardening and reading.

I am author of *Creative Paper Quilts* (Lark Books, 2009); and I am co-author of two self-published books: *Creative Ways with Fiber & Stitch* and *Creative Ways with Books and Journals*. I teach online through Three Creative Studios

Blog: www.stegart.blogspot.com
Websites: www.terristegmiller.com
www.threecreativestudios.com

Nikki Wheeler

Fiber and mixed media art have become a passion for me and save my sanity from the craziness of being Mom. I discovered art quilting while browsing the magazine racks during a rare outing without children. I haven't looked back since. I love playing with color and texture. The softness of wool felt contrasted with shiny glass beads, the way fabric puckers with each stitch, and the serendipitous mixing of wet paint all make my heart sing. Fiber and mixed media allow me the opportunity to play without rules and experiment to my heart's content.

My artistic creations take place in Poulsbo, Washington, where I live with my husband, Adam, and four children, Isabelle, Annaliese, Rosaliegh, and Emitt. I enjoy hiking, sailing, and playing outdoors when I'm not busy with paints or needle and thread.

Blog: www.nikkiwheeler.blogspot.com

Acknowledgments

We want to thank:

our husbands, who have loved us, supported us, listened to us, and tolerated fabric scraps all over the house;

our children and grandchildren, who have stepped on pins and kept smiling;

our families, who have encouraged our creativity and have understood when our projects take time away from being with them;

our friends, who have looked at our work and complimented us even when they didn't know what the heck we were doing;

our neighbors and helpers, who have watched our children, cleaned our houses, covered our obligations, and otherwise enabled us to devote our time to our art projects;

our blog readers, who have faithfully followed our exploits and supported us with enthusiastic comments;

the teachers who've taught us and given us tools and skills with which to work;

the artists who've inspired us and have shown us how to reach for our dreams;

and our editorial team at Lark Crafts, for helping us share our project with you.

Deborah Boschert
Gerrie Congdon
Helen L. Conway
Kirsten Duncan
Terry Grant
Diane Perin Hock
Françoise Jamart
Kristin La Flamme
Karen Rips
Brenda Gael Smith
Terri Stegmiller
Nikki Wheeler

Index

Credits

The following supplied additional photography:
  Page 26: Adam Wheeler
  Page 40: Kelly Goodbun
  Page 80: Ted Rips
  Page 94: Dennis Woodcock
  Pages 109, 112, 114, 118, and 119:
    Stephanie Congdon Barnes
  Page 122: Art La Flamme
  Page 162: Jeffrey Boschert
  Page 167: Claire Boschert